Introduction to Computing—CIS 101

JavaScript 101

Version 3.0, April 2003

Catherine Dwyer, Dr. Narayan Murthy, Dr. David Sachs
School of Computer Science and Information Systems
Pace University

Henry H. Gaylord, III
Consultant
Pace University Computer Learning Center

THOMSON
™
CUSTOM PUBLISHING

Editor: Kenna Roots
Publishing Services Supervisor: Christina Smith
Manufacturing Supervisor: Garris Blankenship
Project Coordinator: Jennifer Flinchpaugh
Graphic Designer: Krista Pierson
Rights and Permissions Specialist: Kalina Ingham Hintz
Marketing Manager: Sara Hinckley

The Adaptable Courseware Program consists of products and additions to existing Custom Publishing products that are produced from camera-ready copy. Peer review, class testing, and accuracy are primarily the responsibility of the authors.

Table of Contents

Introduction to Programming

OBJECTIVES: This material will introduce you to

- Programming languages

- The common elements found in most programming languages

- JavaScript

- Object-based languages

- What software you will need to create and run JavaScript code

About Programming

What exactly is programming? Without it, computers won't work. Who can learn how to program? Even young children, using a special programming language called Logo, are able to write programs. As an introduction to programming and programming languages, we will spend a few weeks learning about JavaScript, a programming language designed to work with Web pages.

A **program** is a set or sequence of instructions entered into a computer to perform work. Programs are written in **programming languages**, such as Visual Basic, Java, C++, or JavaScript. The term **script** is sometimes used to denote a JavaScript program. Programming languages are made up of special terms (called **keywords**), commands, and ways to represent information (data). Programs at first may seem a little strange, but they basically contain English words.

However, the computer cannot carry out instructions written in English. It only understands instructions written in its very own language, **machine code**, or **binary code**. Binary code consists of patterns made up of nothing but 1s and 0s. Can you imagine writing instructions for a computer using just 0s and 1s? Actually, the first programmers had to do this. But then computer scientists figured out a better way. They devised a mechanism to allow programmers to write instructions similar to human language, and then used the computer itself to translate those instructions into machine code.

How does a program get translated into binary code? Well, another program does the job! There are two techniques used to translate a program into binary code. One is called a **compiler**. A compiler looks at all the instructions in the program, and then translates the entire list into a full set of binary instructions. The second type is called an **interpreter**. An interpreter looks at only one instruction at a time, and then translates it into binary code, and the computer executes those instructions. The language we will study, JavaScript, is an interpreted language. When you execute a JavaScript program, your Web browser, i.e. Netscape or Internet Explorer, does the job of interpreting your JavaScript code.

Programming is writing the sequence of instructions that, after being translated into binary code, will allow the computer to complete a task.

Common Elements found in Most Programming Languages

The language we will study in CIS101, JavaScript, has elements common with many other programming languages. Most languages contain ways to represent information (data), statements that examine or transform (change) data, statements that collect (input) data, and statements that format and display (output) data.

The common elements of most languages (including JavaScript) consist of the following:

- variables
- data types
- expressions
- keywords
- statements
- functions

A **variable** is a reference to a storage locations inside main memory (RAM) that contains information relevant to a program. For example, if you used the computer to register for your courses, the program that processed your registration would need a variable to store the number of credits you have registered for. The information stored in variables is in binary format (i.e. only 0s and 1s). The information is also volatile. In other words, just like other information stored in memory, its value in memory can be lost if it is not saved before the machine is turned off.

A **Data Type** is a category of information that a programming language is capable of representing and processing. Although data types vary from language to language, the three found in JavaScript are **Number**, **String**, and **Boolean**. Numbers can represent either integers (whole numbers) or real numbers (numbers with a fractional portion). A String is any sequence of letters, numbers, or other printable characters enclosed within quote marks (either "" or ''). Boolean data can only have two possible values: true or false.

An **expression** is the computer science term for a formula that generates a value. Expressions can contain variables, arithmetic operators like plus (+) and minus (-), and other elements.

A **keyword** or **reserved word** is a word that has a special meaning in JavaScript, and the word cannot be used for any other purpose such as the name of a variable.

A **statement** is a command that can be carried out by a program, such as statements that repeat (for loop and while loop), or statements that examine a condition and branch in different directions depending on the condition (if statement).

A **function** is a part of a program that carries out a specific task or purpose. It is a kind of mini-program. A function has a name, and the function name represents the set of statements inside the function that perform its intended task. So when you use the function name in your code, the statements associated with that name are executed.

About JavaScript

Over the next few weeks you will be learning how to program using JavaScript. The goal for this course is not to make you a programmer. Instead the course's goal is to introduce you to some simple programs, and to give you an appreciation of the work involved in creating a program. Since computer software is constantly changing, understanding how programs are put together will help prepare you to learn new tools.

In 1995 Netscape began to design and implement a new language intended to add interactivity to Web pages. The language was christened "LiveScript" to reflect its dynamic nature, but was quickly renamed JavaScript, a decision that has caused great confusion as to the relationship between Java and JavaScript.

Although their names make them seem related, there is no direct connection between JavaScript and Java, a complex cross-platform programming language developed by Sun Microsystems to write standalone applications or applets attached to HTML pages. JavaScript is also not a subset of Java (meaning that it is not just scaled-down Java with some of the features left out). Although JavaScript is structured in ways that are somewhat similar to Java, there are many differences between the two as well.

JavaScript is a programming language used to create dynamic Web pages. The purpose of JavaScript is to allow code downloaded along with HTML to be executed on the **client**. The client computer is the computer you are sitting in front of when you surf the Web. When you click on a hyperlink, HTML code is copied and transmitted across the Internet from another computer, called the **server**, onto your machine (the client). Your browser, following the instructions contained in HTML, then displays the page. By including JavaScript code with the HTML and allowing it to execute on the client, there is a dramatic decrease in the time consuming back and forth between the client and the server. Before the existence of JavaScript, programs that added interactivity to Web pages ran on the server, resulting in very slow response times. JavaScript is called a "lightweight" programming language because it is not compiled, but is interpreted line by line. This eliminates the need for a compiler, but requires the browser to be JavaScript enabled, which means your browser carries out the job of interpreting the JavaScript code.

You can use JavaScript to:

- Display different HTML depending on whether the browser is Netscape or Internet Explorer.

- Validate user input data prior to sending data to the server for processing.

- Create dynamic effects like animation, scrolling text, swapping of images, and manipulation of layers

- Check for plug-ins being installed.

Some important features of JavaScript:

- It is currently supported by both Netscape and Internet Explorer, although there are many examples of scripts that appear differently depending on which browser you are using.

- JavaScript source code is usually directly embedded in an HTML document.

- JavaScript programs are event driven. As we will learn in Lesson 5, an event is a user action that the computer can respond to. So an event driven program can respond to user events like clicking a button or moving the mouse.

- It is compact and relatively easy to learn.

- It is an object-based scripting language.

- It is an interpreted language (interpreted by the browser).

Object-based Languages

JavaScript is an object-based language. Other object-based languages include Visual Basic and VB Script. An **object** is a "package," a collection of **properties** (variables) and **methods** (functions) all combined under a single name. The properties of an object refer to its characteristics. The methods of an object refer to actions it is capable of executing. For example, imagine that there was an object named car. We could say that the car object possesses several properties: make, model, year, and color, for example. We might even say that car has some methods, or actions it can perform: go(), stop(), and reverse(). Although car is obviously fictional, you can see that its properties and methods all relate to a common theme. Objects are an important component of modern programming languages such as C++ and Java.

Object-based languages have built-in objects already defined and available for use. In JavaScript, some examples include the document object, the location object, and the window object. You will use some of these built-in objects in your programs, beginning in Lesson 1 using the document object to display text. In JavaScript, the set of pre-existing objects is known as the "Document Object Model," or DOM.

The DOM is a hierarchy of objects "built in" to JavaScript. Most of these objects are directly related to characteristics of the Web page or browser. DOM defines the properties and methods for each object. When you write JavaScript code, all the objects in DOM are available for use.

Software You Will Need to Write JavaScript Code in CIS101

Since JavaScript is embedded in HTML code, any HTML editor can be used to write JavaScript. The screenshots in this text will use Notepad, and the browser used will be Internet Explorer 6.0.

Since there are substantial differences between how Netscape and Internet Explorer execute JavaScript, your output might appear quite different from the way it is presented in this book. If you are using Netscape and the output does not seem right, try it with Internet Explorer.

Key Terms and Definitions

- **program** – A sequence of instructions entered into a computer to perform work.
- **programming language** – A set of rules, syntax requirements, and data representation techniques that can be used to create a program, or a set of instructions for a computer.
- **keywords** – Words that are part of a computer language that have been given a specific and precise meaning, allowing the language to generate programs.
- **binary code** – Also known as machine code, it is the series of 0s and 1s that represent information and computer instructions. Computers can only process information and instructions that have been translated into binary format.
- **compiler** – A program that produces binary code (machine code) from instructions written in another programming language. A compiler first examines all the instructions in the input code file, then creates a separate file containing all the machine code needed to execute the program.
- **interpreter** – An interpreter also translates instructions from a programming language into machine code. However, it performs this translation one line at a time. JavaScript is an example of an interpreted language. Your Web browser carries out the task of interpreting your JavaScript code.
- **variable** – Named location in the computer's main memory that stores information in binary format (0s and 1s).
- **data type** – A category of information that a programming languages is capable of representing and processing. The primary data types in JavaScript are Number, representing numeric data, String, representing character data, and Boolean, representing logical data.
- **expression** – A formula that is part of a program that calculates a value.
- **statement** – Command that a computer can carry out.
- **function** – Mini program that carries out a specific task. Also called methods when referring to objects.
- **client** – Computer that requests copies of HTML and JavaScript code for display.
- **server** – Computer that hosts Web pages that may contain JavaScript.
- **object** – Package that is part of a programming language that combines data (properties) and functions or methods that act on the data.

- **properties** – Data that is part of an object.
- **methods** – Functions or actions an object can carry out or complete.
- **Document Object Model** – Hierarchy of built-in pre-defined objects available in JavaScript.

Lesson 1: Writing Your First JavaScript

OBJECTIVES: In this lesson you will be taught how to

- Use the <script> </script> tag

- Insert JavaScript code in a Web page

- Hide your JavaScript code from older browsers

- Use document.write to create output

- Become familiar with built in objects and object notation

- Use embedded HTML to format output

- Display the date and time using the Date object

- Use comments to document code

Preparing to Program

JavaScript code is most often embedded in HTML documents. Since JavaScript code requires the browser to perform special processing, the code is "fenced off" so to speak from the HTML with the `<script>` tag. JavaScript code is placed between `<script>` and `</script>`. JavaScript programs look something like this:

Example

```
<script language="JavaScript">

JavaScript code goes here

</script>
```

Browsers that recognize JavaScript also recognize the special <script> ... </script> tags. Since there is more than one scripting language, the script tag has a language attribute that you set to "JavaScript." The script tag can be inserted in the body of your HTML document or the head of your document. If your JavaScript code will write something directly on the page, it is normally placed in the body section of the document where you want the results to appear. Code that does not write to the page directly, such as code that changes elements or defines variables, is normally placed in the head section. For most of the programs in this course you will insert your code in the body of the document.

Hiding JavaScript from Older Browsers

While this has become less important, very old browsers do not understand JavaScript and will not recognize the script tag. The JavaScript code that is typed between the script tags are just lines of text to those old browsers and will be displayed on the Web page.

To prevent this from happening, a **programming convention** is used that hides the JavaScript inside **comments**. It prevents the JavaScript from being displayed. Of course, it does not solve the original problem, that there are browsers unable to process JavaScript. So this fix will hide your code for those browsers; note that they will be unable to execute it.

It looks something like this:

```
<script LANGUAGE="JavaScript">

<!-- hide (first comment line)

JavaScript code goes here

// finish hiding (last comment line)-->

</script>
```

A programming convention is a common practice used by most professional programmers. Although it is usually a good idea to comply with programming conventions, you are not required to do so by the rules of the language. Comments are parts of programs that document the code but are not executed. They are preceded by a special symbol that tells the broswer not to interpret the text that follows. To hide your code from old browsers, you insert the opening HTML comment code (<!--) just after the opening script tag. Just before the closing script tag, you insert the closing HTML comment preceded by two forward slashes
(// -->).

Using document.write to Display Text

The document.write method is your first JavaScript statement. It writes a line of text to the document. The format for document.write is as follows:

Syntax:
document.write(*"text to be displayed within quotation marks"*)

document.write will display what it finds between the opening parenthesis and closing parenthesis. The characters surrounded by quotation marks are known as a **string**. When the string is displayed, the quote marks are omitted. The purpose of the quote marks is to serve as **delimiters**: symbols that mark the beginning and end of the string. You may also use single quote marks to delimit a string.

As was discussed in the Introduction, document is a built in object in JavaScript. When using objects, you must use **dot (.) notation**. The dot means "belongs to." So document.write("some text") means "use the write method that belongs to the object known as document to display the text found inside the parentheses."

Adding Comments to Your Code

You often want to include information about a JavaScript in the file that contains the code. You may want to include your name for the purpose of handing in an assignment. You sometimes want to explain how a particular section of the code works.

Text that is inside a code file but is not intended to be executed is called a comment. In JavaScript there are two ways to indicate a comment. You can create a single line comment by using //, or create a multi-line comment by using /* and */.

Here are some examples:

```
// everything on this line after the two slashes is a comment
```

or

```
/*
   everything, including what is on this line and below is a comment
   until you encounter the closing symbol, which is
*/
```

These comments only work inside the script tags. If you include them in the HTML section, they will be displayed on the page.

In the Lab

Each week in the lab you will include JavaScript code in your html file and run it using either Internet Explorer ot Netscape. After correctly entering the program and running it without any mistakes, you will start making changes and additions to the code. This is a technique programmers use to learn a new language. Programmers key in a program they know is working, then try to make small adjustments and alterations until they learn enough about the language to write an entire program. Even after learning a language, programmers hardly ever start with a blank page. They usually begin with some code sample close to what they want to accomplish, then make alterations.

Open Notepad and begin a new HTML document. Save it giving it the name lesson0101.html Now type in *exactly* the following code:

```
1   <html>

2   <head>

3   <title>Lesson 01</title>

4   </head>

5   <body>

6   <script language="Javascript">

7   <!--

8   document.write("Hello world!<br>");

9   document.write("This is my first JavaScript.<br>");

10  //-->

11  </script>

12  </body>

13  </html>
```

Your lesson01.html file should look like this:

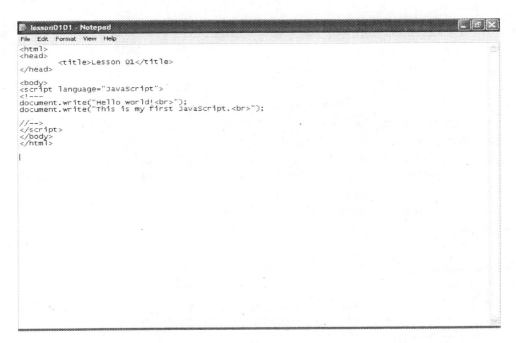

Save the file and open it using either Internet Explorer or Netscape.

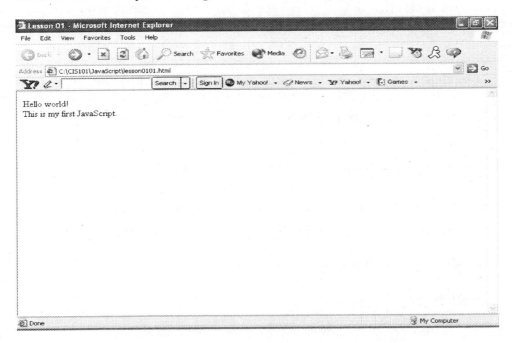

Notice that both lines with document.write end with a semi-colon (;). The semi-colon at the end of a statement is optional. You may also end it with the new line character (by hitting enter). Since other programming and scripting languages end statements with a semi-colon, JavaScript also allows you to put a semi-colon at the end of your statements. You do not need semicolons at the end of statements, and you'll see many examples around the Web of JavaScript code without semi-colons. All you need to do is to start the next statement on a new line.

What to Do if Things Go Wrong

If you do not see the exact same output shown above, then you have made a mistake entering the code. You may have forgotten to save your Notepad file before opening the page with a browser. An error in code is called a bug. Removing errors is called debugging. When you first learn to program, most of the mistakes you make will be keyboarding errors. You might have forgotten the closing quotes on the message or misspelled document.write. Such errors in the format of statements, be it HTML or JavaScript, are known as syntax errors. For the most part, HTML syntax errors are easy to spot and correct: usually the browser just ignores malformed tags and continues on with the page. In contrast, syntax errors in JavaScript code can sometimes be difficult to identify. JavaScript is case sensitive, so "Big" and "big" will not be treated as the same word. This is NOT the case with HTML, so the combination of HTML and JavaScript in one file, with one being case sensitive and the other not is a large source of confusion.

Most Web browsers attempt to assist you in identifying and correcting JavaScript syntax errors. If you try to run your JavaScript in Internet Explorer and it has a syntax error, a window will automatically pop up identifying the error. Unfortunately, the error messages provided by Internet Explorer are not very descriptive, sometimes providing only the line number where the error occurred.

If you use Netscape, a short error message will appear in the status bar (the bottom panel) on the browser window, although that message may be short-lived and easy to overlook. With Netscape, you can generate error messages by entering "javascript:" (the word javascript followed by a colon) in the Location box. This command will invoke the JavaScript Console, which opens in a separate window. The JavaScript Console will identify the line in the HTML document where the syntax error is believed to occur along with a descriptive error message. Usually, this error message will be very helpful in fixing the underlying error.

Building on Your First JavaScript

If you are at this point in the lab, it means you have typed in lesson0101.html, and it is working properly. Do not continue with this section until that is the case.

Let's take a closer look at the first document.write statement:

```
document.write("Hello world!<br>");
```

Notice the <br> tag at the end of the string. If you remember from HTML, <br> forces a new line. It is the equivalent of hitting the enter key. You should find this interesting. It means that not only can you embed JavaScript into HTML, but you can also embed HTML into JavaScript!

Besides <br>, you can use all the other HTML text formatting tags, like headings, the font tags, bold, italic, etc. One important requirement is that the tags must be part of the string. In other words, they must be nested inside the opening and closing quotes that define the string.

Let's start adding more lines.

After line 9 (after the second document.write statement), add the following (if your text is longer than one line you can break it up as indicated below with the backslash):

```
document.write("<h1>This first JavaScript was written by \
(your name)</h1>");
```

You can write in different colors. The next line writes text in maroon. Be careful with the quotes within quotes. The outer quotes are double quotes, the inner quotes (around the word maroon) must be single quotes.

```
document.write("<font color='maroon'>Have a great day!</font><br>");
```

Try writing extra lines using different colors. For more colors to use, see Appendix B, "Named Colors."

Using the Date Object

So far we haven't done anything you couldn't already do with HTML. We just used a different way to display text. Now it is time to spread our wings and to start seeing a little bit of what JavaScript and programming can provide to you. You are probably aware that whenever you turn on your computer, a little clock pops up in the lower right corner showing the current time. If you place your mouse arrow over the time, today's date displays. All computers have an internal clock for the day and time. It is needed by the computer for many purposes, including executing code and saving files. With JavaScript, you can capture the current date and time and display them on your page.

Add the following code:

```
document.write("Today is ", Date(),"<br>");
```

Be careful with the syntax of this statement. Be careful, Date() needs to be capitalized. It will not work if you type it all lower case.

Notice the output has three parts, separated by commas. Type it in exactly as you see it, save your Notepad file, and open your file with a browser.

Your code should display something like this:

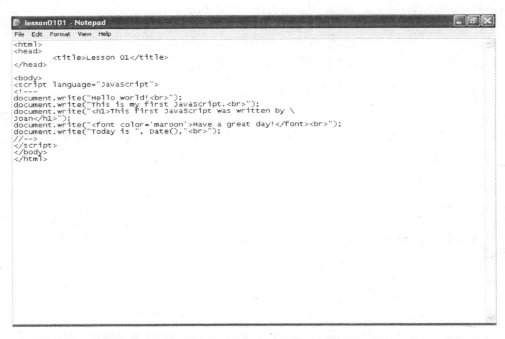

Hit the reload or refresh button of your browser and notice that the time is updated. **Date** is an object that gets the current time and date from your computer's system clock. So each time you reload the page and re-execute that line of code, a new Date object is created.

The syntax of document.write allows you to display a list of things, as long as they are separated by commas. You can keep adding to the document.write statement, as long as each part is separated by a comma. With the comma, the parts are displayed next to each other. If you remove the comma, you will get an error.

Another interesting fact is that the Date object appears differently depending on whether you use Netscape or Internet Explorer. Execute this code using both browsers and notice the differences between the two. This is just a minor example of the compatibility conflicts that exist between Netscape and Internet Explorer. Until this issue is resolved, there will continue to be examples of JavaScript code that do not run the same way with Netscape and Internet Explorer.

Student Modifications

You now have a working JavaScript that uses document.write to display text, uses embedded HTML to format text, and displays the current time and date. Add some more modifications:

- Output a line of text telling us your favorite singer or band.

- Output your email address in your favorite color.

- Output your favorite movie.

- Add a comment within the script tags by using either // or /* and */.

Be sure to always save your Notepad file before testing your code with a browser. If you don't the browser will look at the "old" version of your code, not the version with your most recent changes.

Key Terms and Definitions

- **script tag** – Set of tags (<script> and </script> that enclose JavaScript code.
- **programming conventions** – Standards and practices that are followed by professional programmers but are not required by the syntax rules of a language.
- **comments** – Text that is part of a program file but is not interpreted by the browser. Its purpose is to provide documentation for the code. Comments are indicated in JavaScript by either // or /* and */.
- **document.write** – JavaScript statement that writes text to a page.
- **string** – A word, sentence, or other set of characters, such as letters, numbers, and puctuation marks, surrounded by quote marks.
- **dot notation** – Syntax required when referring to objects. The dot (.) indicates that what follows is part of the object. So document.write means that write is a method that belongs to the object named document.
- **delimiters** – Symbols that act as boundaries for parts of a program. Single and double quotes are both used as delimiters for strings.
- **debugging** – The process of eliminating errors from a program.
- **Date object** – An object available to a JavaScript that contains a specific time and date.

Lesson Summary

In Lesson 1 you learned to write your first JavaScript. You used the script tag to designate JavaScript code within an HTML document, and learned how to hide JavaScript from old browsers. You used document.write to display text. You also used HTML embedded within JavaScript to format text for display. You learned how to use comments to document your code. Finally, you added the Date object to your page to display the current date and time.

Lesson 1 Exercises

1_1.   Write a JavaScript that displays the following double spaced lines:

Hello again!

Your class is CIS101.

What is your name?

1_2.   Write a JavaScript that uses asterisks to display your first initial in block form. For example, the program that Fred writes would output the following:

```
* * * * * * *
*
*
* * * *
*
*
*
```

1_3.   Write a JavaScript program that lists all the courses you are taking this semester. Use a new line and a new color for each course.

Lesson 2: Input and Variables

OBJECTIVES: In this lesson you will learn

- How to include data in your script by using a variable

- How to declare (create) a variable

- How to name a variable (rules for identifiers)

- How to assign a value to a variable using =

- How to combine strings using the + operator, also known as string concatenation

- How to use the prompt statement to collect information from the user

- How to display (output) the contents (value) of a variable

- About string formatting methods

Preparing to Program

A critical feature of programming is the ability to represent data (information). If a computer cannot process information, it is not much use. Programming languages use variables to represent information. A variable is an idea you may remember from algebra: it is a name that stands for a value. Since that value can change (vary) over time, it is called a variable. It does not mean that it has to change, it just means that it may change. In programming, a variable is a container that holds information used by a program. In algebra, you learned that variables like x and y can hold numbers. In JavaScript programs, variables can also hold strings (character data) or Boolean (logical) values.

Declaring Variables

The first step requires that you create a variable. This is called a **variable declaration**. In JavaScript, a variable declaration looks like this:

```
var myName;
```

var is a keyword that indicates this is a variable declaration. This line of code says that "myName" is the name of the variable. In programming, the name of a variable is called an **identifier**. All programming languages have syntax rules that restrict what can be a legal identifier. In JavaScript, the first character must be either a letter or an underscore (_). The remaining characters may include numbers, along with letters or an underscore. You cannot include a blank space or any other special characters like dash (-). You may also not use any JavaScript reserved words as an identifier (see Appendix A for a list of JavaScript reserved words). Identifiers are case sensitive, so"myName" and "MyName" are treated as different identifiers. Mis-spellings caused by the wrong case are usually difficult to spot, so always be careful when creating and using variable names.

Assigning Values to a Variable

Since a variable is a container for a value, you need to know how to put something into that container. You give a value to a variable using this syntax:

```
myName = "Fred";
```

The equal sign is called the **assignment operator**. Notice the value is copied from the right to the left. This is opposite of how you used the equal sign in your math classes. In most programming languages, values are assigned from the right into the left. The opposite direction is an error:

```
"Fred" = myName;
//this is an error, the variable name must be on the left
```

You can also declare a variable and assign it a value at the same time:

```
var anotherName = "Sally";
```

You can also declare a variable and assign it with a numeric value. Here are some examples:

```
var number = 100;

var taxRate = .0825;
```

Using prompt and Variables

An important feature that JavaScript adds to your Web page is interactivity: you can ask users questions, and their answers can determine how the Web page is displayed. The **prompt method** is used to ask a question and to store the answer entered by the user in a variable. Here is the basic syntax for the prompt method:

Syntax:
var varname = prompt("your text","default entry")

You replace *varname* with a variable name, and replace "your text" with the message displayed to the user (usually a question). The second entry, "default entry" sets a default value for the user. Often this is left as "", which is nothing. However, it could be set to something else if you would like to have a default answer ready for the user to see. When the user sees this dialog box, enters a value and presses enter, the string the user has entered is assigned (copied) into the variable. The variable now has the value of the user's input.

The entries inside the parentheses of a method are known as **parameters**. Remember, in the Introduction you learned about the idea of a function or method, which is a mini-program that carries out a specific task. Parameters are information that a method or function uses when carrying out its specialized tasks. You will learn more about parameters, functions, and methods in Lesson 6.

Here is an example of a prompt statement:

```
var myName = prompt("What is your name?", "Enter your name here");
```

When executed, this code displays the following dialog box:

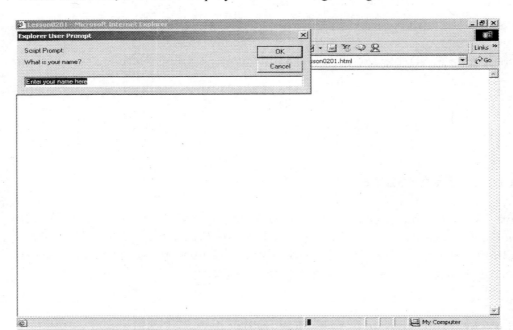

This week in the lab you will use the prompt method to collect information from the user and to make use of it in your programs.

Using Variables with document.write

Once a variable has a value, you can use document.write to display it on a page. It is important to distinguish between the name of a variable and what its contents are. The name of a variable is its identifier. When you refer to a variable in a line of code, you use the name. Variables are stand-ins or placeholders for a value. When the code actually executes and the variable is needed to do something, its value is used. For example, given the following declaration:

```
var myName = "Sam";
```

myName is the name of the variable, and Sam is the value or contents of the variable. When you use a variable in a document.write statement, the contents of the variable are displayed on the page. For example, the statement

```
document.write(myName);
```

displays the name Sam on the page. Notice there are no quote marks surrounding myName. If you were to include quote marks, then the contents of the quote marks, not the contents of the variable would be displayed. The basic rule controlling output is this: characters inside quotes are printed; characters not inside quotes are considered variables, and the value of the variable is printed.

For example:

```
document.write("myName");
```

displays myName on the page, not the name Sam.

Combining Strings Using Concatenation

Concatenation is an operation that combines strings. The + operator, when applied between two strings, combines them into one string. For example:

```
var part1 = "This sentence ";

var part2 = "has ";

var part3 = "three pieces.";

var sentence = part1 + part2 + part3;
```

Once all three parts are combined, the variable sentence has the value "This sentence has three pieces." Notice you need to include blank spaces within the string. If you omit them, the words will run together.

You can also use concatenation to combine strings inside quotes along with variables. For example:

```
var myCar = "Corvette";

document.write("I love to drive my " + myCar);
```

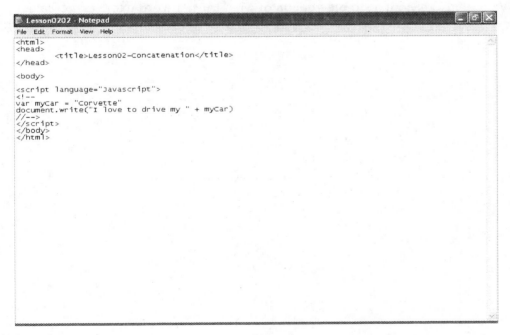

which displays the following:

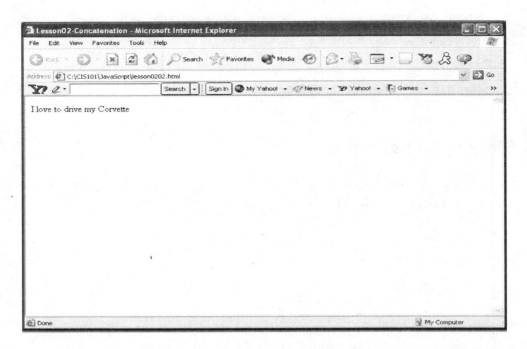

You will use concatenation in this lesson to combine variables containing values input by the user in a display message.

In the Lab

This week in the lab you will add interactivity to your Web pages by introducing variables and user input with the prompt method. This will allow you to customize the appearance of your page. We will also try out a simple version of Mad Libs, a word game that creates mangled sentences.

Open Notepad and begin a new HTML document. Save it giving it the name lesson0201.html Now type in *exactly* the following code:

```
<html>
<head>
        <title>Lesson 2 - Input and variables</title>
</head>

<body>
<script language="Javascript">

<!--

var name=prompt("Please enter your name:"," your name");

document.write("Hello " + name + " !!!<br>");

var yourClass=prompt("What class are you taking?","your class");

document.write("Welcome to <b>" + yourClass + "</b> !!! <br>");

//-->
</script>

</body>
</html>
```

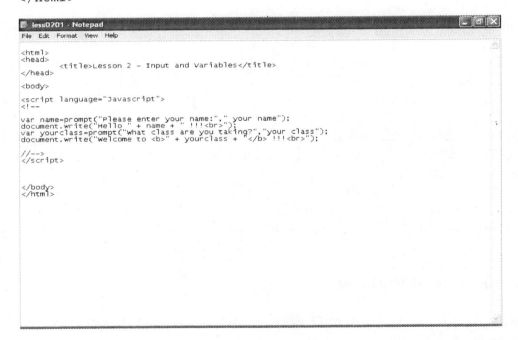

After you have typed in the above code, save your Notepad file and open your page with a browser. If you have any errors, correct your code until you have output that looks like the following:

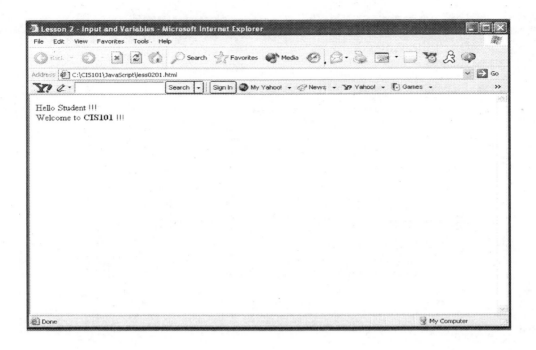

Student Modifications

Make the following modifications to the code:

- In the prompt method set the value of the second parameter to ""', which means empty. This takes away the default entry. Run the code again, and do not input a value, just hit the enter key. What is displayed?

- Create another variable called myMovie. Ask the user to input their favorite movie, and then store their answer in myMovie. Write a document.write statement that displays the variable.

- Use HTML format tags to change the format of a variable. Remember, the HTML tags need to be inside quote marks, so you must use concatenation to do this.

Having Some Fun with Variables

Save your work from the previous exercise. Start a new HTML document using Notepad, save this file as lesson0202.html.

A Mad Lib is a popular party activity where a potentially humorous story is written down, with blanks in the place of some important words. Before reading the story, the storyteller asks others present to fill in those blanks. Those selecting the words are only told the type of word required, and have no other information about the story. This lack of context in selecting words can result in an entertaining story when the words are plugged in the appropriate places.

The following JavaScript code uses variables and the prompt method to create a Mad Lib.

Enter the following code:

```
1   <html>

2   <head>

3   <title>Simple Mad Lib</title>

4   </head>

5   <body>

6   <script language="Javascript">

7   <!--

8   var name = prompt("Give me a name: ","");

9   var verb = prompt("Give me a past-tense verb: ","");

10  var adjective= prompt("Give me an adjective: ","");

11  var sentence = name + " " + verb +

12  " to the museum, and the monkey was " + adjective + ".<p>";

13  document.write(sentence);

14  //-->

15  </script>

16  </body>

17  </html>
```

After entering this code, run it a few times with different words. Check your blank spaces, and be sure the words are spaced properly.

Student Modifications

You have used embedded HTML to change the format of string output. JavaScript also has **string formatting methods** that can simplify your output formatting. For example, add the following code after the first document.write statement (line 13):

```
document.write(sentence.bold());
```

Type this code in and run it. You will see that it displays a sentence in bold. This method performs the task of adding <B> to the front of sentence and </B> to the end of sentence.

Here are some additional string methods:

```
string.blink()

string.fontcolor(colorValue)

string.fontsize(integer1to7)

string.italics()

string.big()

string.small()
```

Try some or all of these methods in your Mad Lib. For example, to use italics, replace string with sentence, i.e.

```
document.write(sentence.italics());
```

If you want to use fontcolor, you will need to include a color as a parameter. Select a color from the list in Appendix B. If you want to use fontsize, you will need to include a number between 1 and 7 as a parameter.

The blink method and fontsize method will only work in Netscape, not in Internet Explorer. This is a mild example of JavaScript that does not work in both browsers. This situation creates serious problems for Web developers.

Key Terms and Definitions

- **variable declaration** – A statement that creates and names a new variable.
- **var** – JavaScript keyword used to create a new variable in a variable declaration.
- **identifier** – The name of a part of your program, like a variable, function or method. In JavaScript, an identifier must begin with either an underscore or a letter, and may only contain letters, numbers or an underscore.
- **assignment operator** – Equal sign (=), used to give (assign) a value to a variable. Values are always assigned from right to left.
- **prompt method** – JavaScript method that asks the user for input and then stores the answer in a variable.
- **parameters** – Data inside the parentheses portion of a function or method. Functions use values in parameters when carrying out their specific tasks.
- **concatenation** – The process of combining strings using the + operator.
- **string formatting methods** – Methods that are used to change the format (appearance) of a string.

Lesson 2 Summary

You learned how to declare and name a variable using the JavaScript rules for identifiers. You also assigned values to a variable with the assignment operator. You queried the user for input, and stored the user's response in a variable with the prompt method. You learned how to combine strings using concatenation and the + operator. You also learned how to display the value of a variable with document.write. Finally you learned how to use string formatting methods to alter the appearance of a string.

Lesson 2 Exercises

2_1.   Write a JavaScript program that uses three variables and three prompt statements. Ask the user to enter their first name, middle name, and last name in separate prompt statements. Then use string concatenation to display the name in the following format:

last name, first name middle name

So if Thomas Francis Jones is the name that is entered, your program will display: Jones, Thomas Francis

Be careful of spaces. Be sure to include any needed spaces within your quote marks.

2_2.   Write a JavaScript program that asks the user to input their name, what city they were born in, and the month of their birthday. Then display that information using document.write.

2_3.   Make your own Mad Lib: In this exercise you will create a Web page that serves as an interactive Mad Lib program. Your page will contain JavaScript code that prompts the user for words to fill in the blanks in a story, and then stores those words in variables. After having read in all of the words, your code should then display the story in the Web page, using the values of the variables where appropriate. For example, here is a start to a Mad Lib:

It was a **adjective** kind of day when **person's name** walked out into the street. The sky was a deep **color** , and **same name** was walking his new pet **animal**...

Making the following substitutions:

- adjective = smarmy
- person's name = Chris
- color = mauve
- animal = gnu

The story would read:

It was a **smarmy** kind of day when **Chris** walked out into the street. The sky was a deep **mauve**, and Chris was walking his new pet **gnu**...

The content of the story can be anything that you like -- be creative! Your story must meet the following conditions, however:

- It must be at least two paragraphs long.
- It must have at least six missing words.
- At least one of the missing words must be used multiple times in the story. For example, the person's name was used twice in the sample story above.
- The page should have a title, centered at the top, that includes your name.

Lesson 3: Variables and Arithmetic

OBJECTIVES: In this lesson you will learn

- To use the arithmetic operators +, -, *, / to solve problems

- To use the assignment operator(=) to give a numeric value to a variable

- How operator precedence controls the order in which an expression is calculated

- To use the alert method to display informatio

- How to use the Math object in calculations

Preparing to Program

All programming languages have the ability to carry out arithmetic operations. The name computer has its root in the machine's original purpose, which was to compute values that are difficult or impossible to calculate by hand.

In JavaScript, arithmetic operations are carried out with the arithmetic symbols you use in math class. These symbols are called **arithmetic operators**. There are other types of operators in JavaScript that you will learn about in subsequent lessons.

JavaScript provides the following commonly used binary arithmetic operators. Binary means there are two values used, with the operator in between them.

The addition operator +

The binary + is the addition operator: **A + B** yields the sum of A plus B.

The subtraction operator –

The binary - is the subtraction operator: **A - B** yields the difference A minus B.

The multiplication operator *

The binary * is the multiplication operator: **A * B** yields the product A multiplied by B.

The division operator /

The binary / is the division operator: **A / B** yields the dividend of A divided by B.

Simple Expressions

As you learned in the Introduction, an expression is the computer science term for a formula that returns a value. In JavaScript and other languages, an expression can be a combination of variables, **literals**, and arithmetic operators. A literal is a number itself, like 4, 92.7, etc.

Given the following variable definitions:

```
var num1 = 6;

var num2 = 3;
```

Here are some expressions and their values:

```
num1 * 2 yields 12

num1 + num2 yields 9

num1/num2 yields 2
```

Expressions can be used in combination with the assignment operator to give a value to a variable. Consider the following:

```
var length = 5;

var width = 6;

var area;
```

The formula for calculating the area of a rectangle is:

area is equal to length times width

If we were to write this as JavaScript, it would look like this:

```
area = length * width;
```

So if length is 5 and width is 6, then area has a value of 30. Remember that assignment always goes from right to left. So first length is multiplied times width, and then the answer is assigned to the variable area.

Expressions with More than One Operator

Expressions can also have more than one operator. For example, the formula for calculating the perimeter of a rectangle is length plus the width times 2. So in JavaScript, the code to calculate the perimeter would look like this:

```
var length = 5;

var width = 6;

var perimeter;

perimeter = length + width * 2;
```

Although this looks right, it will not produce the right answer. The correct answer is length + width (11) times 2, which yields 22. The expression above yields length (5) plus width times 2(12), or 17. Why does it end up with the wrong answer?

It has to do with a rule of mathematics called **operator precedence**. When an expression has more than one operator, the computer has to decide which operation goes first. The computer can only carry out one operation at a time. Even though the time it takes to carry out that operation is blindingly fast, it still does one thing at a time. The computer must select the correct order in which the operations are carried out. This order is called operator precedence.

It determines which operations have precedence, or go first. It is the same order defined in your math classes when you took algebra. Multiplication and division take precedence over addition and subtraction. If more than one operator is on the same level, for example if you have addition and subtraction in the same expression, then those operations are carried out from left to right through the expression.

How can we fix our problem with calculating the perimeter? We want to override the standard order and force the addition to take place first. To do this we use parentheses. Just like in algebra, the operations inside parentheses have higher precedence and therefore are carried out first.

Here is a corrected formula for perimeter:

```
perimeter = (length + width) * 2;
```

This will produce the correct answer, because length will be added to width before it is multiplied by two. Notice you have to explicitly include the '*' symbol for multiplication; otherwise you will have an error.

Operator Precedence Table

This table summarizes the operator precedence information you will need in order to perform basic arithmetic in JavaScript. The operations are carried out in order from top to bottom:

Type of Operator	Example of Operators
Parentheses (Overrides others)	( )
Multiplication, Division	*, /
Addition, Subtraction	+, -
Assignment	=

The alert method

In Lesson 1 we learned how to display output using document.write. There are other ways in JavaScript to display output. The technique you will use in this lesson is the **alert method**. The alert method displays a small pop up window, sometimes called a message box.

It looks like this:

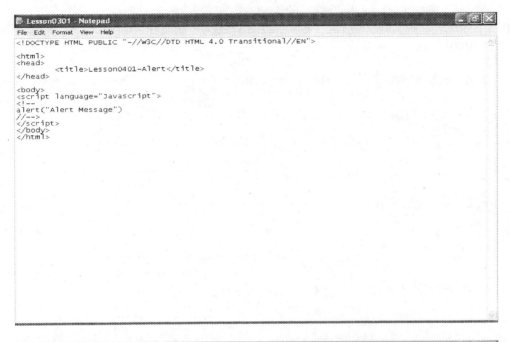

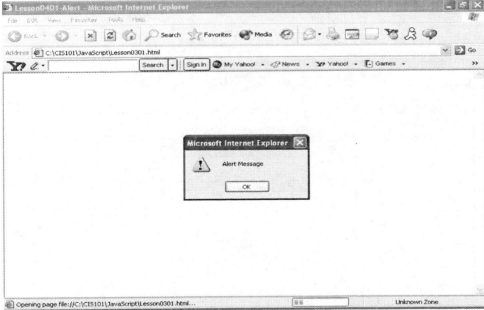

Syntax:
`alert`("*message*")

The alert box will display the specified message. When the user clicks the OK button, the alert box is removed.

In the Lab

This week in lab you will use JavaScript to solve problems using variables, arithmetic operators, assignment, and the alert statement.

Open Notepad and begin a new HTML document. Save it giving it the name lesson0301.html

Now type in *exactly* the following code:

```
1   <html>
2   <head>
3   <title>Lesson 3: Variables and Arithmetic</title>
4   </head>
5   <body>
6   <script language="Javascript">
7   <!--
8   var length=10;
9   var width = 5;
10  var area = length * width;
11  document.write("The length of the rectangle is ",length,"<br>");
12  document.write("The width of the rectangle is ",width,"<br>");
13  document.write("The area of the rectangle is ",area,"<br>");
14  //-->
15  </script>
16  </body>
17  </html>
```

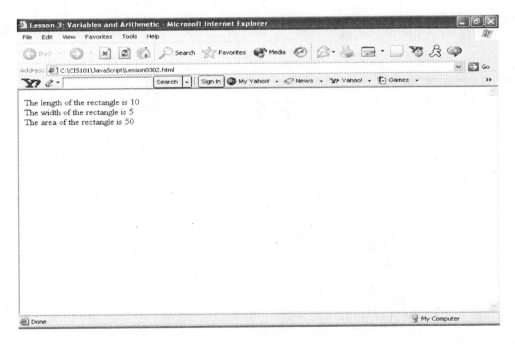

```
Lesson0302 - Notepad
File  Edit  Format  View  Help
<html>
<head>
      <title>Lesson 3: Variables and Arithmetic</title>
</head>

<body>
<script language="Javascript">
<!--
var length=10;
var width = 5;
var area = length * width;
document.write("The length of the rectangle is ",length,"<br>");
document.write("The width of the rectangle is ",width,"<br>");
document.write("The area of the rectangle is ",area,"<br>");
//-->
</script>
</body>
</html>
```

After accurately entering the code above, save your Notepad file and open your page with a browser. You should see the following output:

The length of the rectangle is 10
The width of the rectangle is 5
The area of the rectangle is 50

After you have run the program and obtained the correct output, try the program again with different numbers. Change the values for length and width to other numbers, including numbers with a fractional value, like 2.7 or 5.6, and run the program again.

Now add the following code, which will calculate the perimeter and display its value using the alert method. Insert this code after line 13 (the third document.write statement):

```
var perimeter = 2*length + 2*width
```

```
alert("The perimeter is "+perimeter);
```

```
You should see the following output:
```

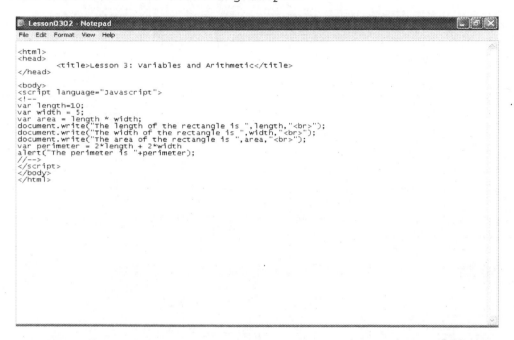

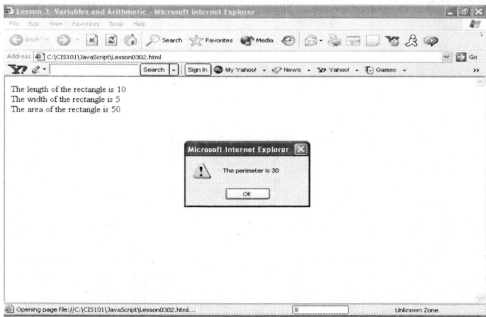

Student Modifications

- Change the first document.write statement which displays the length to an alert statement, then run the code. Notice that this alters the appearance of the text. The subsequent document.write statements do not appear until the user clicks OK.

- Add the variables base and height, and assign them values. Add a variable triangleArea and code to calculate and display the area of a triangle. The formula for the area of a triangle is:

```
triangleArea = 1/2*base*height;
```

- Add a variable radius and assign it a value. Add variables circleArea, circleCircumference, and code to calculate and display the area and the circumference of a circle. The formula for the area of a circle is:

```
circleArea = radius*radius*Math.PI;
```

The formula for the circumference of a circle is:

```
circleCircumference = 2*radius*Math.PI;
```

Math.PI is an example of a **defined constant** that is part of the **Math object**. Math.PI is defined with a value of 3.141592653589793, or the approximate value of π. Math is a built-in object which has a large number of properties and methods to handle mathematical computations.

Key Terms and Definitions

- **arithmetic operators** – The symbols + (plus), - (minus), * (multiplication), and / (division) that are used in JavaScript to carry out arithmetic.
- **literals** – Numbers like 6, 9, 2.33, that can be used in an expression or to assign a value to a numeric variable.
- **operator precedence** – The order that the browser follows when evaluating expressions that contain more than one operator. The basic order is parentheses, multiplication or division, then addition or subtraction.
- **alert method** – The JavaScript method that displays a pop up window with a message and an OK button. The alert window remains visible until the user clicks OK.
- **Math object** – A built-in JavaScript object with a large number of properties and methods useful for carrying out mathematical calculations.
- **defined constant** – A number, like the value of π, that has be defined and assigned a value. Programmers can use defined constants in expressions to solve problems.
- **Math.PI** – A defined constant, part of the Math object, that holds an approximate value for π.

Lesson 3 Summary

In Lesson 3 you learned about arithmetic operators and how expressions are evaluated by the browser using operator precedence. You learned how to use JavaScript to solve problems, like calculating and displaying the area of common shapes like a rectangle and triangle. You used the alert method as an alternate way to display output. Finally you used the Math object and defined constant Math.PI to calculate and display the area and circumference of a circle.

Lesson 3 Exercises

3_1.   Write a JavaScript program that converts a distance in miles into a distance in kilometers. One mile is equal to 1.60935 kilometers. If you multiply the number of miles times 1.60935, you will calculate the number of kilometers. Declare miles as a variable and give it a value. Declare kilometers as a variable. Use the formula above for converting miles to kilometers to assign a value to kilometers. Display the results in an alert box. Include the original number of miles and the calculated distance in kilometers in the message displayed in the alert box.

For example, if the number of miles is 5, then your program should produce the following output:

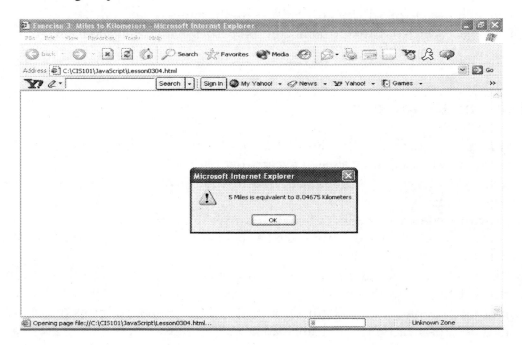

3_2.　Your pulse rate is the number of times your heart beats per minute (usually about 70 per minute for an adult and higher for children.) Write a JavaScript program with a variable to represent your age in years. Determine the number of minutes in a year: 60*24*365, and multiply this by your age in years. Then determine the approximate number of times your heart has beaten by multiplying this result by 80, an average rate that takes into account the faster rate for children. Display the results using an alert box.

For example, if your age is 18, this is what your program should produce:

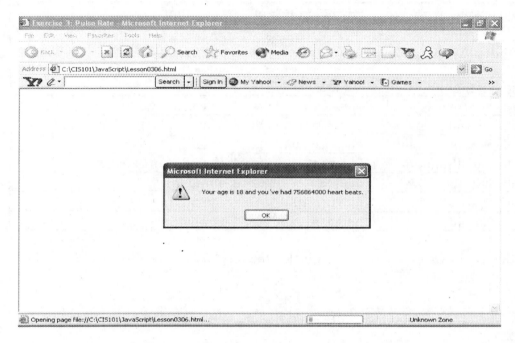

3_3.　Write a JavaScript program to convert Celsius temperature values to Fahrenheit. The formula for the conversion is:

Fahrenheit = 9 * Celsius/5 + 32

Use different variables for Celsius and Fahrenheit, and display the results in an alert box.

3_4.   Here is a list of some of the methods available in the Math object:

Method syntax	Arguments	Returns
Math.abs(num)	number	absolute value of num
Math.ceil(num)	number	The least integer greater than or equal to num
Math.cos(num)	number (angle in radians)	cos(num)
Math.floor(num)	number	The greatest integer less than or equal to num
Math.log(num)	number >0	ln(num)
Math.max(num1,num2)	both are numbers	The greater of num1 and num2
Math.min(num1,num2)	both are numbers	The smaller of num1 and num2
Math.pow(num1,num2)	both are numbers	num^{num2}
Math.round(num)	number	Rounded off integer
Math.sin(num)	number	sin(num)
Math.sqrt(num)	number ≥0	√num
Math.tan(num)	number	tan(num)

Use document.write statements to display the results of some of these Math methods. For example, the code

```
document.write("absolute value of -4 is = ",Math.abs(-4),"<P>")
document.write("square root of 30 is = ",Math.sqrt(30),"<P>")
```

displays the following results:

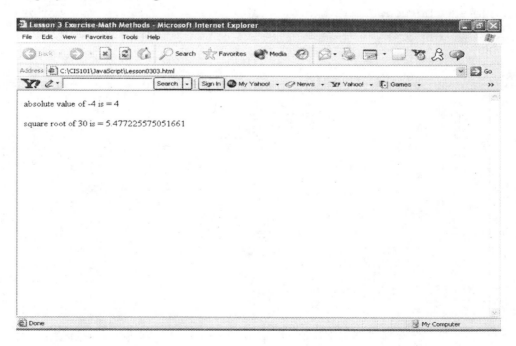

Lesson 4: Formatting Input Data for Arithmetic

OBJECTIVES: In this lesson you will learn about

- Data types

- String data versus numeric data

- How input data (from the prompt method) is stored as a string

- Why you need to format input data for arithmetic

- How to use built in JavaScript functions to format input data for arithmetic (parseInt, parseFloat, and eval)

Preparing to Program

In Lesson 3 we learned how to use arithmetic to solve problems in JavaScript. In this lesson, you will take that one step further by using the prompt method to collect user data for your calculations. This is more complicated, because JavaScript (and most other languages) store input data in the form of a string, i.e. character data. In the Introduction, you learned that JavaScript has three basic data types, or formats for information: Numeric, String, and Boolean. Information in the form of a string cannot be used in arithmetic: it must be converted (formatted) into the numeric format that the computer can use to carry out arithmetic.

This might seem strange to you. Think of it this way: you have been using HTML to format your output. Sometimes you use bold; sometimes you use different colors. In a similar way, you need to format the data ***coming into*** your program. If you want to use input data to carry out arithmetic, you need to convert it to a numeric format.

The following example illustrates the problem. It uses the prompt method, which you used in Lesson 2, to collect information from the user. (Filename is less04_ex1.html):

```
<script language="Javascript">

<!--

var num1=prompt("Enter a number:","0");

var num2 = prompt("Enter a second number:","0");

document.write("num1 = ",num1,"<br>");

document.write("num2 = ",num2,"<br>");

document.write("num1 + num2 is equal to " + num1+num2,"<br>");

//-->

</script>
```

If you run the above code, and enter 5 for num1 and 6 for num2, you get the following output:

```
num1 = 5

num2 = 6

num1 + num2 is equal to 56
```

Hopefully you find this to be wrong! Whenever you use prompt to collect data, you need to be careful. Often it will not cause a problem since JavaScript will automatically convert the input string to a number when a numeric operation (such as '*' or '-') is applied. However, addition is a problem since the '+' operator may be interpreted as string concatenation.

In the above code, we want the computer to add those numbers together. But + can also mean string concatenation. So when the browser sees two strings joined by a plus sign (i.e. num1+num2), it carries out concatenation.

You can solve this problem by explicitly converting num1 and num2 into a numeric format. To do this you can use the **parseFloat method**. The word "parse" in English means to extract. So parseFloat extracts a float from a string. This method converts a string into a number. Then the browser sees two numbers joined by a plus sign, and carries out addition. Here is the same example as above using parseFloat. (Filename is less04_ex2.html):

```
<script language="Javascript">

<!--

var num1=parseFloat(prompt("Enter a number:","0"));

var num2 =parseFloat(prompt("Enter a second number:","0"));

document.write("num1 = ",num1,"<br>");

document.write("num2 = ",num2,"<br>");

document.write("num1 + num2 is equal to ",num1+num2,"<br>");

//-->

</script>
```

If you run the above code, and enter 5 for num1 and 6 for num2, you get the following output:

```
num1 = 5

num2 = 6

num1 + num2 is equal to 11
```

This code produces the correct result.

JavaScript Methods that Convert Strings into Numbers

JavaScript provides several functions that convert strings into numbers.

The method parseFloat(*string1*) returns *string1* as a decimal number, that is a number with a fractional portion.

If *string1* does not start with a number, parseFloat() gives an error message.

If *string1* starts with a number followed by some other characters, parseFloat() converts the number part of the string and ignores the rest.

Examples

parseFloat("235")   returns the number 235

parseFloat("23.45")   returns the number 23.45

parseFloat("23.45abc")   returns 23.45

parseFloat("ab34.46")   results in an error

The method **parseInt**(*string1*) returns *string1* as an integer.

If *string1* does not start with a number, parseInt() gives an error message.

If *string1* starts with digits followed by some other characters, parseInt() converts the number part of the string and ignores the following non-numeric part.

parseInt() always returns a whole number.

Examples

parseInt("235")   returns the number 235

parseInt("23.45")   returns the number 23

parseInt("23.45abc")   returns 23

parseInt("ab354")   results in an error

You can also convert strings to numbers with the method **eval**(*string1*), where the *string1* is a numeric expression in the form of a string. The eval method evaluates *string1* and returns its value.

Example

```
<script language="Javascript">

<!--

a = "3 +2*5"

document.write(a,"<P>")

document.write(eval(a))

//-->

</script>
```

The first line output is: 3+2*5

The second line output is : 13

In the Lab

This week in lab you will use JavaScript methods to convert user input from string format to numeric format, and then carry out calcuations using arithmetic operators and expressions.

Open Notepad and begin a new HTML document. Save it giving it the name lesson0401.html Now type in *exactly* the following code:

```
1   <html>

2   <head>

3   <title>Lesson 4: Formatting Input Data For Arithmetic</title>

4   </head>

5   <body>

6   <script language="Javascript">

7   <!--

8   var ageString;

9   var age;

10  age = parseFloat(prompt("Please enter your age:",""));

11  document.write("You are " + (age * 7) + " in dog years!");

12  //-->
```

```
13  </script>

14  </body>

15  </html>
```

The above program calculates your age in dog years. Try it out a few times to confirm that it is calculating the correct result.

Student Modifications

- You can also calculate the age of a dog in human years. Prompt the user to enter the age of their dog. Use parseFloat to convert the input value to a numeric format and store it in a new variable dogAge. Then convert to human years with the following formula:

```
dogToHumanYears = ((dogAge - 1) * 7) + 9
```

and display the result.

- Do other conversions, from cat years (cats live about 20 years) to human years. Look on the Internet for other possibilities: giant Redwood trees (500 to 700 years), Galapagos Turtles (200 years), etc.

Key Terms and Definitions

- **parseFloat method** – JavaScript method that converts a string into a numeric decimal format, i.e. a number that has a fractional portion.
- **parseInt method** – JavaScript method that converts a string into an integer format, i.e. a format that is a whole number.
- **eval method** – JavaScript method that converts a string in the form of an expression into its numeric value.

Lesson 4 Summary

In Lesson 4 you learned that JavaScript stores data input with the prompt method as a string. You also learned that data in string format cannot be used to carry out arithmetic. You learned that JavaScript provides several methods to convert strings into numbers. They are parseFloat, which converts a string to a decimal number, parseInt, which converts a string to an integer, and eval, which converts an expression in the form of a string into a numeric value.

Lesson 4 Exercises

4_1.   Sales Tax Calculator: Write a JavaScript program that calculates the sales tax and total price of an item. Assume a sales tax rate of 8%, which means you will multiply the cost of the item by .08 in order to calculate the tax amount.

Use prompt and parseFloat to ask the user to input the item's cost and convert it to a numeric format. Declare a variable salesTax and use the formula above to calculate the sales tax amount. Declare a variable totalCost, add the item's cost plus the sales tax amount, and store it in totalCost. Output the Item cost, tax amount, and total cost on separate lines in the form of a receipt.

Enhancements:
- Don't assume a tax rate of 8%. Instead, ask the user to input the tax rate in the form of a decimal, i.e. .05, .03, etc., and use this tax rate for the calculations.
- Display the tax amount in a different color.
- Depending on the price of an item, you may end up with a tax amount that takes up more than 2 decimal places. Use the following code to round the tax amount to two decimal places:

```
var taxAmtRnd = Math.round(taxAmount*100);

taxAmtRnd = taxAmtRnd/100;
```

This code multiplies the tax amount by 100, rounds it off, then divides by 100. This drops any extra decimal places from the tax amount. The rounded tax amount is in the variable taxAmtRnd.

4_2.   Miles per gallon Calculator: Write a JavaScript program that calculates miles per gallon. Use parseFloat and prompt to ask the user to input the total number of miles driven and to store that number in numeric format. Use parseFloat and prompt to ask the user to enter the number of gallons consumed. Calculate the miles per gallon with the following formula:

milesPerGallon = milesDriven/gallonsConsumed

Display the answer using the alert method.

4_3.   Write a JavaScript program to assist a cashier in determining the total value of coins in a coin tray. Using parseInt and prompt, ask the user to input the number of quarters, dimes, nickels, and pennies and to store the input in separate variables. Set the default entry equal to "0", so the user can hit enter and skip to the next prompt if they do not have any of a particular coin. Then add up the total value by multiplying the number of quarters by .25, the number of dimes by .1, the number of nickels by .05, and the number of pennies by .01. Display the final total using the alert method.

Lesson 5: Introduction to Events

OBJECTIVES: In this lesson you will learn about

- Event driven programming

- Events and event handlers

- The onClick event handler for hyperlinks

- The onClick event handler for buttons (forms)

- The mouse event handlers onMouseOver and onMouseOut

Preparing to Program

A popular feature of the World Wide Web is its interactive nature. When you access a Web page, you don't just view the page, you interact with it. You click on links and buttons to change pages, make windows pop up, or enter information in forms and view responses based on your entries. In these and many other ways, Web pages are responsive to your actions. In other words, Web pages are **event driven**, reacting to **events** that you initiate such as mouse clicks or keyboard entries.

An event is an action by the user. Some examples of events are:

- clicking a button;
- moving the mouse pointer over a hyperlink;
- changing the contents of a text box;
- entering or leaving a text box.

Event driven programs use events as triggers for program execution. Events signal requests and commands from the user that the program carries out by executing code.

In this lesson, you will learn to use JavaScript to control event driven Web pages. You will use buttons and hyperlinks to initiate actions, and you will learn how you can use JavaScript to make a Web page respond to mouse events to display different images.

Event-driven Programming

In previous lessons you wrote JavaScript programs that collected user input and produced an output page. These programs executed statements in a predetermined pattern: asking a user for data at certain points, and computing results based on the data. Once your program started, it was in complete control of its execution. It ran to completion and then stopped.

Event driven programs are different. With Web sites it is difficult to know exactly what the user will do and when. For example, a Web page may present a number of clickable images, text boxes, and check boxes that the user can choose to click. There are many possible sequences of clicks that the user can perform. Perhaps he or she will choose to click a link that shows a new page, then return later to the original page and click a button that submits data to a remote server. Or perhaps the user will instead click an image that starts an applet. On large, complex pages there are many possibilities presented to the user.

It is very difficult, if not impossible, to write code that predicts the sequence of actions the user might select in such a situation. Instead, it is far simpler to write a separate piece of code for each of the possible things that the user can do. When the user chooses an action, such as clicking a button, the corresponding piece of code can be executed. In this way, the code is set up to respond to the actions of the user, instead of running to completion by itself. The control of the order of execution is in the hands of the user, rather than the program.

Events and Event Handlers

In event driven Web pages, user actions determine the course of code execution. User actions are events, and the separate sections of code that responds to events are called **event handlers**. An event handler is a predefined JavaScript keyword. It is a special attribute that is associated with hyperlinks, buttons, and other elements of a Web page. Event handlers always begin with the word **on**. Examples of event handlers include **onClick**, **onMouseOver**, and **onMouseOut**.

Event driven JavaScript waits for your Web page visitor to take a particular action, such as placing the mouse arrow over an image, before it reacts by executing code. The key to coding event driven JavaScript is to know the names of events and how to use them.

It is important to understand that events happen to a particular button, link, or other component on the Web page. You can say that an event *belongs* to that component. This should make sense to you. If you click the mouse on a blank part of a Web page, there is no response. If you click a button on the page, then *that button's* event handler executes.

So where do you insert this event handler code? Since an event belongs to a Web page component, its event handler code should be placed with the component itself. In this lesson, you will write event handlers for hyperlinks and buttons, and you will see that the event handler code is part of the definition of the links and buttons you include in your Web page.

onClick Event Handlers and Links

This first example of an event handler is part of a hyperlink. You have been clicking hyperlinks since the first day you saw a Web page. The default action of a hyperlink is to go to a new Web site. Using the JavaScript event handler onClick, this code instead produces an alert message. (Filename is less05_ex1.html):

```
1   <html>

2   <head>

3   <title>onClick and Hyperlinks</title>

4   </head>

5   <body>

6   <h1>Example of an onClick Event Handler</h1>

7   <a href="#" onClick = "alert('This is what it does!');">Click this
    link!</a>

8   </body>

9   </html>
```

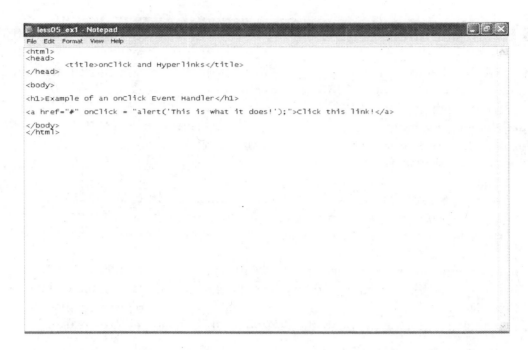

When you run this code and click the link, the following message appears:

All the relevant code for the event handler is in line 7, where the link is defined. The symbol "#" is HTML code that tells the browser to stay on this page. Next is the keyword onClick. Notice it is inside the anchor tag, and there are no script tags. They are not needed with event handlers.

The syntax for the onClick event handler is as follows:

Syntax:
```
onClick="JavaScript statement(s);"
```

The event handler code you write is placed inside a pair of quote marks. Let's take a closer look at the code for this particular event handler:

```
onClick = "alert('This is what it does!');"
```

Notice there are two sets of quotes. The outer set of double quotes serves as delimiters (boundaries) for the event handler. Nested inside the alert method is another pair of single quotes. These serve as delimiters for the message string. You often have to nest quotes with event handlers, and it is easy to make a mistake that causes your code not to run.

Follow these rules when using quotes with event handlers:
- alternate pairs of double quote marks with single quote marks
- inner quote marks must be paired up (nested) within the enclosing quotes. For example:

"This is an error 'caused by overlapping" quote marks.'

The quotes should really be placed this way:

"This is the 'right way' to nest quotes inside each other."

Also notice that the alert statement ends with a semicolon. This enables you to add additional JavaScript code after the alert, performing multiple actions in response to a click event rather than a single JavaScript statement. For example: (Filename is less05_ex2.html).

```
1   <html>

2   <head>

3   <title>Multiple Alerts</title>

4   </head>

5   <body>

6   <a href="#" onClick="alert('one'); alert('two'); alert('three');
    alert('four'); alert('five');">Click this link</a>

7   </body>

8   </html>
```

This link's onClick event handler produces five alert messages. This is possible because each alert is separated by a semi-colon. But it should be apparent that this method quickly gets inconvenient and messy. In the next lesson you will learn a better way to write event handlers with complex logic and multiple statements. You will learn how to write a function to handle the event. Since a function is a separate section of code, it is easier to put multiple event handler statements within a function.

onClick Event Handlers for Buttons

Buttons are elements of HTML forms. You declare a button by including an input tag with type set to button within form tags. Buttons also have onClick event handlers with the same syntax as links.

Here is an example of JavaScript code that displays an alert message when the user clicks the button. (Filename is less05_ex3.html):

```
1   <html>

2   <head>

3   <title>onClick and Buttons</title>

4   </head>

5   <body>

6   <form>

7   <input type="button" value="Click Me" onClick="alert('You clicked a
    button');">

8   </form>

9   </body>

10  </html>
```

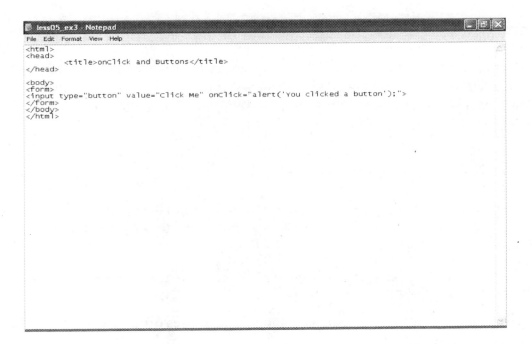

Here is what the output looks like:

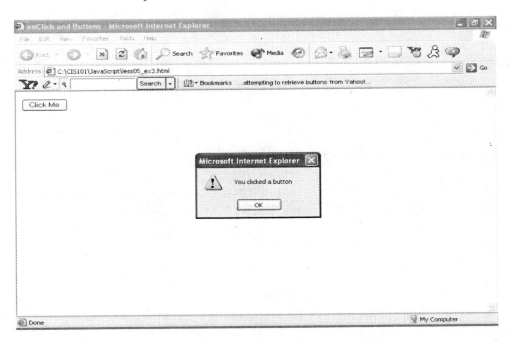

Notice the syntax for the onclick event handler is the same as for hyperlinks. You need to include the keyword onClick within the definition for the button. You need to enclose the code for the event handler within double quotes. You need to use single quotes for any interior quotes. You should also terminate statements with a semi-colon to allow you to add extra statements. Now that you see how the click event works, we will explore events and event handlers associated with moving the mouse.

Mouse Events

Links can respond to other events, such as those triggered when the user moves the mouse. Two event handlers you will learn about are **onMouseOver** and **onMouseOut**. Moving the mouse arrow over a link triggers onMouseOver. The onMouseOver event handler has a syntax similar to the onClick method:

Syntax:
```
onMouseOver="JavaScript statement(s);"
```

Just like the onClick event handler, you need to insert this code in the definition for the link. You also need to enclose the JavaScript statements within quote marks. Here is a sample onMouseOver event handler for a link:

```
<a href="#" onMouseOver = "alert('You are over this link');">Mouse Over
Link</a>
```

The onMouseOut event is triggered when the mouse arrow moves off of a link. Here is the syntax for onMouseOut:

Syntax:
```
onMouseOut="JavaScript statement(s);"
```

Here is a example for onMouseOut:

```
<a href="#" onMouseOut = "alert('You are now off this link');">Mouse
Out Event</a>
```

Mouse Event and the Window Status Bar

A common functionality for onMouseOver is to use it to write a message in the window status bar, the thin grey bar at the very bottom of your browser window.

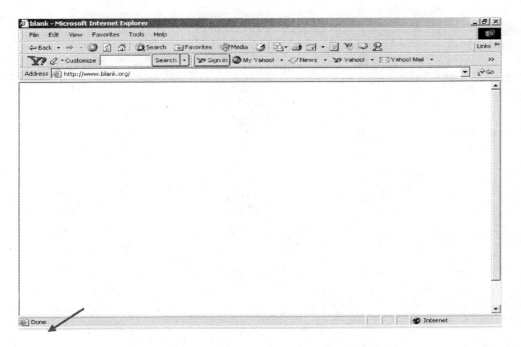

JavaScript code can change the status bar by accessing the **window** object, a JavaScript built in object. You have already used the document object and document.write to display text, now you will learn how to use the **window** object. The built-in JavaScript window object has many useful properties, including the status property. By assigning a value to the status property, you change what is displayed in the status bar in your browser. Here is an example:

```
window.status = "Welcome to CIS101!"
```

This code displays the message "Welcome to CIS101" in the status bar. Remember the dot notation that is required when accessing parts of an object. This notation, window.status, means that status is a property of the window object.

Here is a program that changes the status bar using onMouseOver. (Filename is less05_ex4.html):

```
1   <html>

2   <head>

3   <title>onMouseOver Example</title>

4   </head>

5   <body>

6   <center>

7   <h1> onMouseOver and Status Bar</h1>

8   <a href="#" onMouseOver="window.status='over first';

9   return true;">First</a>

10  <p>

11  <a href="#" onMouseOver="window.status='over second';

12  return true;">Second</a>

13  <p>

14  <a href="#" onMouseOver="window.status='over third';

15  return true;">Third</a>

16  <p>

17  </center>

18  </body>

19  </html>
```

Notice the return true statement after the window.status command. This extra code is needed to keep the new message visible. When the user places the mouse arrow over one of these links, it triggers the onMouseOver event handler. The statement "return true" prevents the URL from appearing in the status bar (this is the default behavior). If you do not include "return true", then your message will be briefly displayed and then quickly replaced by the URL.

You will use these two events, onMouseOver and onMouseOut, together in the lab to produce an image swap. You are not required to use them together. You can use each one by itself, or even combine them with the onClick event handler.

Here is a link with all three event handlers:

```
<a href="#"       onMouseOver = "window.status = 'now you are over';"
                  onMouseOut = "window.status = 'now you are out';"
                  onClick = "alert('now you have clicked');">
                  Link With Three Event Handlers</a>
```

You also have onMouseOver and onMouseOut events associated with buttons. Here is a similar example coded for a button:

```
<form>

<input type="button" value="click" onMouseOver = "alert('over');"
onMouseOut="alert('out');" onClick = "alert('click');">

</form>
```

Even with these simple events, you now have a lot of power in your hands. Users are constantly moving the mouse. To see how often this event handler is used, just visit a few Web sites and notice what happens when you move the mouse. Does the appearance of the page change? What happens to the status bar? In the lab you will shortly learn to write the code that carries out these things yourself.

In the Lab

This week in the lab you will use JavaScript to write event-driven programs, responding to the click event, and the onMouseOn and onMouseOver events. When writing JavaScript code in this lesson, you will not include the <script> tags. The browser "knows" that anything that is part of an event handler is written in a script.

Open Notepad and begin a new HTML document. Save the file with the name lesson0501.html.

Now type in *exactly* the following code:

```
1   <html>

2   <head>

3   <title>Click Event With Links</title>

4   </head>

5   <body>

6   <center>

7   <h1>Click your favorite color:</h1>

8   <a href="#" onClick="document.bgColor='red';">Red</a>

9   <p>

10  <a href="#" onClick="document.bgColor='blue';">Blue</a>

11  <p>

12  <a href="#" onClick="document.bgColor='green';">Green</a>

13  <p>

14  </center>

15  </body>

16  </html>
```

When you run this code, it allows you to select different background colors for your document. Run your program and test that each color works properly. If you have problems, confirm that you have double quotes defining both the beginning and end of the onClick event handler, and that you use single quotes for the colors. Be especially careful about spelling event handlers and property names. Pay close attention to what letters are upper case and what letters are lower case.

Let's look in more detail at the code that changes the background color:

```
onClick="document.bgColor='red';"
```

bgColor is a property of the document object, and it stands for background color. It is the JavaScript equivalent of the <body bgcolor> tag, although in JavaScript the property name is case sensitive. The other body tag attributes also have JavaScript equivalents. Here is a table of the properties and a description of what they do:

Document property	Description
fgColor	color of text
linkColor	color of link the user has not yet visited
vlinkColor	color of link user has already visited
alinkColor	color of link user clicks

You can use JavaScript statements to change the value of these properties as well. Consider the following:

```
document.fgColor = 'yellow';
```

This code changes the color of the text to yellow. The difference between using HTML to set these values and using JavaScript is that you can allow the user to select, through events and event handlers, the way the page is displayed. This makes pages containing JavaScript dynamic and interactive compared with those created only with HTML.

Student Modifications

- Refer to Appendix B and select three additional colors. Add three new links along with onClick event handlers that change the bgColor property to the new colors. Test the added colors to ensure they are working properly.

- For each color (you should now have six), select a contrasting value for the fgColor property (document.fgColor). The fgColor property controls the color of the text. Insert a second statement for each onClick event handler changing the fgColor property to a selected contrasting color. Be very careful adding this additional statement. Be sure that the first statement ends with a semi-colon and that you terminate the entire event handler with closing double quotes. Here is a sample link that sets the bgColor property to red and the fgColor property to yellow:

```
<a href="#" onClick="document.bgColor='red';
document.fgColor='yellow';">Red</a>
```

Run your code and experiment with your color combinations. Select some that look nice together. Also try to get find a worst possible combination. What happens when bgColor and fgColor are the same? Save your file with its modifications.

The onClick Event Handler and Buttons

Now you will learn to use the click event with buttons.

Open Notepad and begin a new HTML document. Save it giving it the name lesson0502.html

Now type in *exactly* the following code:

```
1   <html>

2   <head>

3   <title>Click Event With Buttons</title>

4   </head>

5   <body>

6   <h1>Click the button to see the greeting</h1>

7   <center>

8   <form>

9   <input type="button" value="Hello" onClick="alert('Welcome to
    CIS101');">

10  <input type="button" value="Goodbye " onClick="alert('So long, come
    back soon!');">

11  </form>

12  </center>

13  </body>

14  </html>
```

After you have entered this code, test both buttons to ensure they work properly. Then add a third message of your own choice.

Swapping Images with Mouse Events

A common use of mouse events is for swapping images. The following code swaps a red arrow for a blue arrow as you move the mouse over a link. Save your earlier work and begin a new Web document and save it with the name lesson0503.html. Obtain from your instructor the two image files needed, redArrow.gif and blueArrow.gif, and save them in the same folder as your HTML document lesson0503.html.

Now type in the following code: <html>

```
1    <head>

2    <title>Creating A Simple Rollover</title>

3    </head>

4    <body bgcolor="white">

5    <h1>Creating A Simple Rollover</h1>

6    <p>

7    <h2>Roll your mouse on top of the blue arrow and then away from it
     and watch the arrow color change!</h2>

8    <center>

9    <a href="#" onMouseOver="document.arrow.src='blueArrow.gif';"
     onMouseOut="document.arrow.src='redArrow.gif';">

10   <img src="redArrow.gif" width="300" height="82" border="0"
     name="arrow"></A>

11   </center>

12   </body>

13   </html>
```

After entering this code, try it out. You should see the arrow change from red to blue and back to red as you move the mouse arrow over and away from the link. If it is not working properly, check for the common causes of errors:

- misspelled keywords – be sure to check upper and lower case letters
- mismatched quote marks - you need double quotes for the event handler, single quotes for the image file
- misspelling the image file name
- the image file not in the same folder as is your html file

After you have the code working, read this section that explains how it works. Even though this code swaps two images, there is only one image tag in above code. Here is how it works. Before you can use JavaScript to swap an image, you first have to assign that image a name. Notice the following code inside the image tag:

```
name="arrow"
```

This assigns the name arrow to the image. The code that actually swaps the image is in the event handlers:

```
<a href="#" onMouseOver="document.arrow.src='blueArrow.gif';"
onMouseOut="document.arrow.src='redArrow.gif';">
```

Notice the syntax document.arrow.src. This is dot notation, once again. It means that arrow is part of document, and src (source) is part of arrow. The swap is executed by changing the source property of the arrow image that is part of the document. If the mouse is over the link, the arrow is blue. If the mouse arrow moves off the link, the arrow is red.

Once you have this code working, try it out with other pairs of images. You can also add another statement to the event handlers to change the bgcolor property when you change the image.

Key Terms and Definitions

- **event-driven programming** – Programming method used to create interactive Web pages. Event driven programming executes code in response to user actions.
- **event** – Action by the user, such as clicking a mouse, that triggers a response from a Web page.
- **event handler** – Code that a Web page executes in response to an event by the user.
- **onClick event handler** – JavaScript keyword that is used in code to define how a Web page responds to a click event intiated by a user.
- **onMouseOver event handler** – JavaScript keyword that is used in code to define how a Web page responds to the event triggered when the user places the mouse arrow over a link.
- **onMouseOut event handler** – JavaScript keyword that is used in code to define how a Web page responds to the event triggered when the user places the mouse arrow away from a link.
- **window.status** – Status is a property of the JavaScript built-in object window. It controls what is displayed in the browser's status bar.
- **document.bgColor** – bgColor is a property of the JavaScript built-in object document. It controls the background color of the page displayed by the browser.
- **document.fgColor** – fgColor is a property of the JavaScript built-in object document. It control the foreground color of the page displayed by the browser. The foreground color controls the color of any text displayed.

Lesson 5 Summary

In Lesson 5 you learned that event-driven Web pages respond to user actions, and allow the user to control the order of program execution through the use of events and event handlers. You learned how to write code for the onClick event handler for both hyperlinks and buttons. You learned how to write the onMouseOver and onMouseOut event handlers as well. You used these events to allow the user to alter the appearance of the page by changing the background color, the foreground color, and the contents of the status bar. Finally you learned to perform an image swap using mouse events with a hyperlink.

Lesson 5 Exercises

5_01. The following table lists the distance from the sun to the planets in our solar system.

Planet	Mean Distance from Sun (millions of miles)
Mercury	36.0
Venus	67.1
Earth	92.9
Mars	141.5
Jupiter	483.5
Saturn	886.7
Uranus	1782.7
Neptune	2794.3
Pluto	3666.1

Create a Web page and add nine buttons to your page, one for each planet. Remember you need to use the form tags when using buttons. Set the caption of each button to a name of a planet (i.e. value= "Mars"). When the user clicks a planet, display an alert message with its distance from the sun.

5_02. Remember that HTML allows an image to act as a hyperlink through the following syntax:

```
<a href="some link here"><img src="somefile.gif"
border="0"></a>
```

If you use this code to turn an image into a link, the image can now respond to mouse events.

Create a Web page and include a picture of yourself. Turn your picture into a link using the syntax above. Use the stationary link syntax (href="#"). When the mouse arrow goes over your picture, use the onMouseOver event handler to display an alert box with the message "Get that mouse arrow off my face!"

5_03.   The following code uses the onMouseOver event handler to write to the status bar. (Filename is less05_ex4.html):

```
1   <html>

2   <head>

3   <title>onMouseOver Example</title>

4   </head>

5   <body>

6   <center>

7   <h1> onMouseOver and Status Bar</h1>

8   <a href="#" onMouseOver="window.status='over first';
    return true;">First</a>

9   <p>

10  <a href="#" onMouseOver="window.status='over second';
    return true;">Second</a>

11  <p>

12  <a href="#" onMouseOver="window.status='over third';
    return true;">Third</a>

13  <p>

14  </center>

15  </body>

16  </html>
```

If you run this code and place your mouse arrow over "First," the status bar changes to "over first." However, when you move the mouse arrow off the link, the status bar still displays the now outdated message. To fix this you need to reset the status bar to blank (' ') when the mouse arrow is moved away from the link. Add the event handler onMouseOut that sets window.status equal to blank (' '). You will need to use two single quotes in order to do this, i.e.

```
onMouseOut="window.status=' ';"
```

5_04.   Another interesting property of the window object is location. You can point the window to a new Web page by setting a new value to the location property, i.e. the code

```
window.location='http://cnn.com'
```

connects this window to the Web site for CNN.

Find three or four Web pages related to each other. For example, find the Web sites of four news organizations, like www.cnn.com, and www.nytimes.com. Create a Web page and add three or four buttons to the page. Use each button to connect to a different news service Web site by altering the window.location property in each button's onClick event handler.

Lesson 6: Introduction to Functions

OBJECTIVES: In this lesson you will learn about

- Functions

- Why functions are useful

- How to declare a function

- How to use a function

- Why functions are used with event handlers

Preparing to Program

As programs become larger and more complex, they need to be structured and organized. This is true for most things. Think about how textbooks are organized. There are chapters, sections, and units that break up the material into smaller pieces. Smaller pieces are easier to understand and create.

The same idea applies to programs and programming languages. As programs grow in size, they need to be broken up into smaller pieces. These smaller parts are called functions, methods, sub-routines, or sub-programs, depending on the programming language. JavaScript uses the term **function** or **method** to describe these smaller units of code. There is no formal definition to describe when you use the term function or method. In general, methods are associated with objects, and functions are free standing, not connected to a particular object.

A function or method is a unit of code that performs a specific, well defined task. You have already used these JavaScript functions:

- document.write – to write text to a Web page
- alert– to display a message inside a small window with an OK button
- prompt– to collect input from the user and store it in a variable

There are many other JavaScript functions that you can use. These functions give additional power and utility to your code. Functions are collected into **function libraries**. Much of the effort of learning a programming language centers on becoming familiar with what function libraries are available for use.

Why Functions Are Useful

Besides giving some structure and organization to your code, functions make programming much easier. As you program more, you will find that you are often repeating and rewriting similar sets of instructions again and again. Using functions means you do not have to repeat your code. Instead of copying the code over and over again, you can place it inside a function and then use the function repeatedly.

In JavaScript, functions are often used as event handlers. Recall that when you write code for an event handler, you must insert the code inside the definition of the link, button, or other Web element that generates the event. If you write more than one or two statements, it gets very messy. The preferred technique is to place the statements inside a function, and to then execute the function when the event handler is triggered.

Defining Functions

This lesson will show you how to define and use your own functions. The code that defines your function is normally placed in the head section of your HTML document. This allows your function to be loaded with the page and available for use when needed.

You begin by first declaring your function. A **function declaration** is similar to a variable declaration. In the first line of your function, your declare it as a function, give it a name, and indicate if it accepts any **parameters**. To declare a function, you start with the key word *function,* followed by its name, and then a set of parentheses:

```
function functionname()
```

The same rules for variable names also apply to function names. Function names must begin with a letter or underscore (_), and can only contain letters, numbers, and underscore. Function names, like variable names, are case sensitive.

We will briefly defer the discussion of parameters. After the first line, there is a ***required*** open curly brace {. After the opening brace, you place all the code to be executed when the function performs its task. The end of the function is marked with a closing curly brace }.

The general structure of a function is

```
function function-name ()
{
JavaScript statements
go here
} // end of function-name
```

The left brace defines the beginning of the function body, and the right brace indicates the end of the function body.

Parameters and Functions

Functions carry out tasks. Often, it is useful to have data available for the function to use when performing its task. Data is provided to a function by using parameters. You have already used parameters with JavaScript methods like alert and document.write. When you use these methods, you provide information within the parentheses that the function uses to carry out its task.

The syntax for a function with parameters is as follows:

```
function functionname(parametername1, parametername2,...)
```

These parameters are special variables made available to the function. Each parameter name must be a legal variable name, and that name must be unique within the list of parameters. Notice that each name is separated by commas. A function can have zero or more parameters. Even if a function has no parameters, the parentheses after the function name are required.

Return Statements and Functions

A common task that functions perform is some kind of calculation. For example, you could write a function that calculates the sales tax on a purchase. Once the function determines its result, it returns the result back to the main part of your program. This is accomplished by using the keyword **return** statement. The syntax of the return statement is straightforward:

```
return variablename;
```

For example, to return the calculated sales tax amount, you include the following code in your sales tax function:

```
return salesTaxAmount;
```

Calling Functions in JavaScript

There are two code sctions required when you use functions. The first part, described above, declares the function. It has specific syntax requirements, and it is usually placed in the head section of your Web document.

The second part is the code that actually allows you to use the function. In programming languages, using a function is referred to as a **function call**. A function is not executed until it is called. It is available on standby for use, but will not be executed unless a statement inside your page calls that function.

The syntax for a function call is also straightforward. If the function has no parameters, than the function call looks this:
```
functionname();
```

For example, here is a small JavaScript program that calls a function without parameters. (Filename is less06_ex1.html):

```
1   <html>
2   <head>
3   <title>Function without Parameters</title>
4   <script language="javascript">
5   function myFunction()
6   {
7   alert("HELLO");
8   }
9   </script>
10  </head>
11  <body>
12  <form>
13  <input type="button"
14  onClick="myFunction();"
15  value="Call function">
16  </form>
17  </body>
18  </html>
```

When executed, this code displays the following:

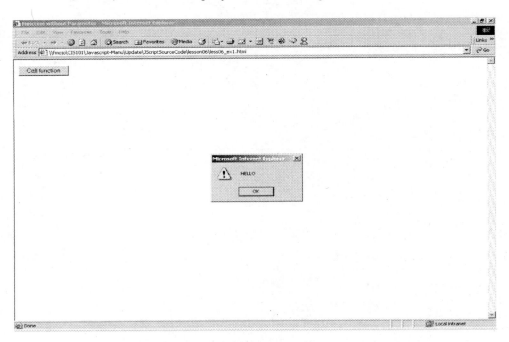

The function is named myFunction. It is declared within the head section of the Web document. Notice that you still must use the script tags for the function declaration. The function call is within the event handler onClick. Once you click on the button, the event handler calls the function. myFunction executes, and it displays an alert message. Although this is a simple example, it demonstrates the basic syntax of function declarations and function calls.

Calling a Function with Parameters

When calling a function that has parameters, the function call must include the exact number of parameters as required by the function. If the function has two parameters, the function call must include two parameters.

A function call with parameters takes the following form:

```
functionname(parametername1, parametername2, ...);
```

The code above can be modified to add a parameter to myFunction. Here is what the revised program looks like. (Filename is less06_ex2.html):

```
1   <html>

2   <head>

3    <title>Function with Parameter</title>

4   <script language="javascript">

5   function myFunction(message)

6

7   {

8   alert(message);

9   }

10  </script>

11  </head>

12  <body>

13  <form>

14  <input type="button"

15  onClick="myFunction('hello with a parameter');"

16  value="Call function">

17  </form>

18  </body>

19  </html>
```

Notice the following changes. myFunction now has a parameter called message inside its parentheses. The alert statement uses the parameter message when it produces its message box. And the function call now has a value inside its parentheses; that value is passed to the function.

When this code executes, the following is displayed:

With this version, myFunction is defined with one parameter. The value of that parameter is used by the alert statement. The function call is once again triggered by the onClick event handler. The words 'hello with a parameter' are now passed along to the function when it is called by the event handler. If you change the words inside the function call, the result of the function will be different.

Function Calls and Event Handlers

Functions are often used in conjunction with event handlers to respond to user events. One simple reason is that event handler code looks cleaner and is easier to understand if you use a function. To demonstrate this, consider this example. The following code does not use a function to handle an event. (Filename is less06_ex3.html):

```
1   <html>

2   <head>

3    <title>Event Handler Without Function</title>

4   </head>

5   <body>

6   <form>

7   <input type="button"

8   onClick="alert('one');alert('two');alert('three');alert('four');"
```

```
9   value="Alerts Without Function">

10  </form>

11  </body>

12  </html>
```

This crams all the statements between a set of quotes next to the event handler. If you make a mistake, it can be difficult to spot. If you wanted to add anything, you could start to have problems. The solution is to use a function. (Filename is less06_ex4.html):

Here is the same program re-written using a function:

```
1   <html>

2   <head>

3   <title>Event Handler With Function</title>

4   <script language="Javascript">

5   <!—

6   function someAlerts()

7   {

8   alert('one');

9   alert('two');

10  alert('three');

11  alert('four');

12  }

13  //-->

14  </script>

15  </head>

16  <body>

17  <form>

18  <input type="button"

19  onClick="someAlerts();"

20  value="Alerts With A Function">

21  </form>

22  </body>

23  </html>
```

Instead of cramming many statements on one line, the event handler has a single statement, the function call itself. When the event is triggered, the event handler calls the function, and the function displays the four alert statements. In the lab you will use functions that will be used by event handlers to respond to user events.

In the Lab

This week in lab you will learn to write your own functions and use them in your code.

Open Notepad and begin a new HTML document. Save it giving it the name lesson0601.html Now type in *exactly* the following code:

```
1   <html>
2   <head>
3   <title>The Don't Click Function Demo</title>
4   <script language="Javascript">
5   <!—
6   function sayOuch()
7   {
8   document.bgColor = "red";
9   alert ("ouch!!");
10  document.bgColor = "white";
11  } // end of function
12  //-->
13  </script>
14  </head>
15  <body>
16  <center><h1>Don't Click Function</h1>
17  </center>
18  <hr>
19  <center>
20  <form name = myForm>
21  <input type = button
22  value = "really, don't click me."
23  onClick = "sayOuch();">
24  </form>
25  </center>
26  </body>
27  </html>
```

If you enter the previous code correctly and run it, you will see the following output:

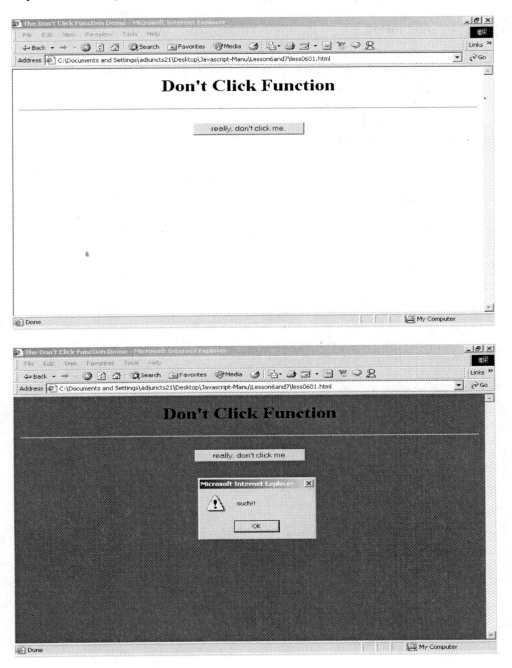

Notice that you place the function declaration in the head section of your html document, inside the same script tags you have already used. Notice also the function call from the onClick event handler. When the user clicks the button, the function sayOuch() is executed. The function sayOuch() changes document.bgColor to red, displays an alert box with the word 'ouch!', and then changes the document.bgColor back to white.

Student Modifications

- Change the colors used by the function.

- Add a second button and second function that use different colors and a different message. Test it out using both buttons.

Using a Function with a Parameter

Save your work from the previous exercise. Start a new HTML file, and name it lessson0602.html. This example will show you how to use a function with a parameter. Now type in *exactly* the following code:

```
1   <html>

2   <head>

3   <title>Event Handlers and Functions</title>

4   <script language = "Javascript">

5   <!-- Hide script from older browsers

6   function saySomething (message) {

7   alert (message)

8   }

9   //end hiding script from older browsers -->

10  </script>

11  </head>

12  <body bgcolor=white>

13  <h2>Using a Function With a Parameter</h2>

14  <h2>Famous Quotes <br>(Click a button to see what they have to say!)

15  </h2>

16  <hr>

17  <form>

18  <input type="button" value="Lincoln"

19  onClick="saySomething ('Four score and seven years ago...')">

20  <input type="button" value="Kennedy"

21  onClick="saySomething ('Ask not what your country can do for
```

```
22 you...')">

23 <input type="button" value="Nixon"

24 onClick="saySomething ('I am not a crook!')">

25 </form>

26 </body>

27 </html>
```

If you click the Lincoln button, the following is displayed:

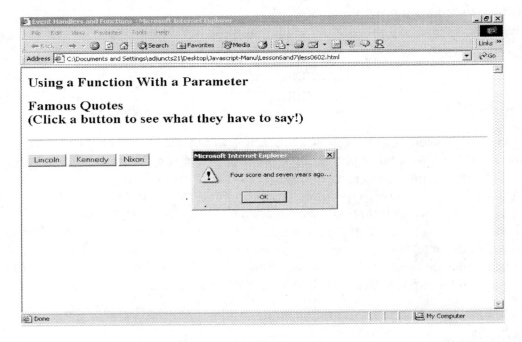

This example also uses a function to display a message. Notice the same function can be used for all three buttons. By using a parameter, the message displayed can change.

Student Modifications

- Add another button for another famous quote. Use the existing function, and display the message by using the parameter.

- Add a second parameter, and use it to display a second alert box with the name of the person being quoted. You need to add the second parameter into the function declaration. Then you have to add another alert statement in the function, and change *all* the function calls to include the second parameter.

Key Terms and Definitions

- **function or method** – A set of statements that carries out a specific task.
- **function libraries** – Collections of functions available for programmers to use in their programs.
- **function declaration** – Required syntax that defines how the function carries out its task.
- **parameters** – Special variables that are declared within parentheses along with the function. Parameters contain data the function uses in carrying out its task.
- **return statement** – Return is a JavaScript key word that allows a function to send or return a value to the main program.
- **function call** – A statement that uses the function. Code inside functions does not execute without a function call.

Lesson 6 Summary

You have learned that when programs grow in size, it is important to organize and structure them by breaking them into smaller pieces. In JavaScript, these smaller pieces are called functions or methods. A function is a set of statements that carries out a specific task. You can create your own functions by first writing a function declaration in the head of your Web document. The function declaration gives the function a name, lists its parameters, and inside a set of curly braces contains the statements that will execute when the function carries out its task. In order to use the function, you write a function call. The function call consists of the function name plus any required parameters. Finally, you learned that functions are often used with event handlers to organize and simplify a Web page's response to a user event.

Lesson 6 Exercises

6_1.   Create a Web page that does the following. Write a function combineWords(word1,word2) that displays both words (i.e. the words in the parameters) in an alert box with a space between them. Be sure to place the function declaration in the head section of your document, inside script tags.

Then in the body section, add script tags and include JavaScript code that prompts the user to input two words. Store this input in two variables, word1 and word2. Then write a function call to combineWords, passing the value's input to the functions. Hint: use concatenation inside the function to combine the words.

6_2.   Here is the code for less0501.html from Lesson 5:

```
1   <html>

2   <head>

3   <title>Lesson 05: Introduction to Events</title>
4   </head>

5   <body>

6   <center>

7   <h1>Click your favorite color:</h1>

8   <a href="#" onClick="document.bgColor='red';">Red</a>

9   <p>

10  <a href="#" onClick="document.bgColor='blue';">Blue</a>

11  <p>

12  <a href="#" onClick="document.bgColor='green';">Green</a>

13  <p>

14  </center>

15  </body>

16  </html>
```

Rewrite this code using functions for each event handler. Name your functions
clickRed(), clickBlue(), and clickGreen(). Place each function in the head section of
your Web page. Change the onClick event handler for each link so that it calls the
appropriate function. Inside each function, include code to change document.fgColor
to a different value. Also include a statement that uses window.status to display the
name of the color that was linked.

6_3.   Rewrite exercise 4_2 using a function milesPerGallon that calculates and displays the
miles per gallon in an alert box. Here is the original description for the exercise:

Write a JavaScript program that calculates miles per gallon. Use parseFloat and a
prompt to ask the user to input the total number of miles driven and store it in
numeric format. Use parseFloat and a prompt to ask the user to enter the number of
gallons consumed. Calculate the miles per gallon with the following formula:

milesPerGallon = milesDriven/gallonsConsumed

Write a function milesPerGallon(milesDriven, gallonsConsumed). It should take the
values passed in the parameters milesDriven and gallonsConsumed to calculate the
miles per gallon. In the function, use an alert statement to display the result.

Then in the body section of your Web page, prompt the user to enter the total number of miles driven and store the user's answer in the variable milesDriven . Also prompt the user to enter the number of gallons consumed and store the user's answer in the variable gallonsConsumed. Then write a function call to milesPerGallon, passing the values in milesDriven and gallonsConsumed to the function.

Lesson 7: If Statement and Comparison Operators

OBJECTIVES: In this lesson you will learn about

- Branching or conditional statements

- How to use the comparison operators: `==`, `!=`, `<` `<=`, `>`, `>=`

- How to use if and if … else to evaluate conditions and make decisions

Preparing to Program

It is often useful to take a course of action depending on some circumstance. It does not always rain, so you do not always take an umbrella with you. But if it is raining, or is expected to rain soon, you would be wise to take your umbrella.

Programs and Web pages are often faced with a similar situation. For example, we have already discussed the fact that a Web page with JavaScript works differently depending on whether you are using Netscape or Internet Explorer. So it is useful for a Web page to determine if you are using Netscape or Internet Explorer, and to execute different code depending on the result.

In programming, code that asks a question and executes different paths depending on the answer is known as a **branching** or **conditional statement**. Picture in your mind a branch in the shape of a fork: you can go either left or right. The term conditional statement implies that execution depends on a condition. If the condition has a certain value, do this; if it does not, then do something else.

This lesson will teach you how to use the **if** and **if .. else statement**. The if and if … else statements are examples of a conditional statement. Conditional statements work in the following way: they ask a question, then execute certain code depending on the answer. In JavaScript, and in most other programming languages, conditional statements ask a question by using **comparison operators**. Before we discuss the syntax of the if statement, we need to explore the topic of comparison operators.

Comparison Operators

Comparison operators are used to make comparisons. For example you can compare two variables to test if they are equal. Other comparisons are available (see the table below). For each of the comparison operators, the result of the comparison is always either **true** or **false.** True or false values are known as **boolean values**.

Here is a table that describes the comparison operators available to you in JavaScript:

Operator	Meaning	Comments
==	equal	True if the two operands are equal; false otherwise.
! =	not equal	True if the operands are not equal; false otherwise.
<	less than	True if the left operand is less than the right operand; false otherwise.
<=	less than or equal to	True if the left operand is less than or equal to the right operand; false otherwise.
>	greater than	True if the left operand is greater than the right operand; false otherwise.
>=	greater than or equal to	True if the left operand is greater than or equal to the right operand; false otherwise.

These operators should already be familiar to you. You have used them in math class to make comparisons.

Examples

Here are some simple examples that demonstrate how to use comparison operators:

Assume: **a = 7** **b = 4** **c = 10**	**Assume:** **name = "Pace"** **state = "NY"** **address = "1 Pace Plaza"**
a < b is false. **a < b+c** is true. **a*b >= 2*c** is true **a+b != 0** is true **a+b+c == 21** is true	**name <= state** is false **name > address** is true **state == address** is false

The if Statement

The if statement is an example of a conditional or branching statement. The if statement works in the following way: it asks a question, normally by using comparison operators. Depending on the answer, it will execute certain code.

Here is the general syntax for the if statement:

```
if ( condition )

{
 JavaScript statements go here
}
```

If the *condition* is true, the *statements* between { ... } will be executed. If the *condition* is false, the *statements* between { ... } will be skipped. The group of statements between { ... } is called the **if block**. Any statements may be placed in this if block, including additional if statements.

Recall that you used curly braces { and } to define the boundaries for a function in the last lesson. Notice also, that the *condition* can only be true or false. In programming, you can only ask yes/no or true/false questions. If you ever played the game 20 Questions, you know it can be quite a challenge to figure out something by only using yes/no questions. This is one of the restrictions that can make programming a difficult task.

Example

```
if (city == "New York")

{
 state = "NY"

 areacode = "212"

 document.write(city,state)

}
```

If the condition **city == "New York"** is true, all of the statements in the if block will be executed. If the city does not match "New York," none of the if block's statements will be executed.

The if ... else Statement

An **if** statement can also have an **else** clause that executes if the condtion is false. This enables a two-way branch so that one block of statements can be executed when the condition is true, and a second block of statements can be executed if the condition is false.

Syntax for if ... else:
```
if (condition)

{

statementgroup1

}

else

{

statementgroup2

}
```

If the *condition* is true, *statementgroup1* (the if block) will be executed and *statementgroup2* will not be executed; otherwise (when the condition is false), *statementgroup1* will not be executed and *statementgroup2* (the **else block**) will be executed.

Example

```
if (city == "New York")

{

state = "NY";

areacode = "212";

}
else
{

state = "CT";

areacode = "203";

}

document.write(city,state);
```

In this example, if city has the value "New York," then the two statements in the if block will be executed and the statements in the else block will not. If city does not have the value "New York," the statements in the if block will be skipped and the statements in the else block will be executed. This is why the if … else statement is called a branch.

Note

When the **if** block and/or the **else** block have only one statement, the curly braces can be omitted. If the braces are omitted, the statement *must appear* on the same line as the if and/or else. For example:

```
if (city == "New York") state = "NY"
else state = "CT"
document.write(city,state)
```

---

if Statement and Browser Detection

Recall at the beginning of the lesson we mentioned that it is useful for a Web page to determine what broswer is being used to view the page. This can be done with an if … else statement. Here is what the code looks like. (Filename is less07_ex1.html):

```
var browserName = navigator.appName;

if (browserName == "Netscape")
{

alert("You are using Netscape");

}
else if (browserName == "Microsoft Internet Explorer")
{

alert("You are using Internet Explorer");

}
```

If you insert this code in a Web page then open it with Internet Explorer you will see the following message:

If you open it with Netscape, you will see this message:

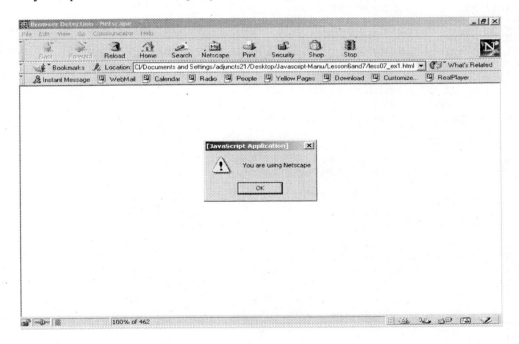

What do you think will happen if you open this page with a browser other than Netscape or Internet Explorer?

This code works in the following way. The variable browserName is assigned a value from navigator.appName. The navigator object is another example of a JavaScript built in object. The navigator object stores information about what browser is being used. The appName property stores the name of the browser being used. Another navigator property available is appVersion, which indicates what version number of the browser is being used.

In the if statement, browserName is compared for equality with the string "Netscape" by using the == operator. If the comparison is true, then the alert box announces you are using Netscape. If the comparison is false, it makes a second comparison. It now compares browserName with the string "Microsoft Internet Explorer." If they are equal, the alert box announces you are using Internet Explorer. Many Web pages use JavaScript to determine what browser you are using and then they execute different code depending on the result.

In the Lab

In this lesson you will learn how to use comparison operators and the if and if .. else statements.

Open Notepad and begin a new HTML document. Save it giving it the name lesson0701.html Now type in *exactly* the following code:

```
1   <html>
2   <head>
3   <title>Simple If Statement</title>
4   </head>
5   <body>
6   <h1>Using an If Statement</h1>
7   <script language="Javascript">
8   <!--
9   var number=parseInt(prompt("Enter a number",""));
10  if (number > 10)
11  {
12  alert("The number was greater than 10");
13  }
14  //-->
15  </script>
16  </body>
17  </html>
```

If you run this code and enter the number 11, you see this result:

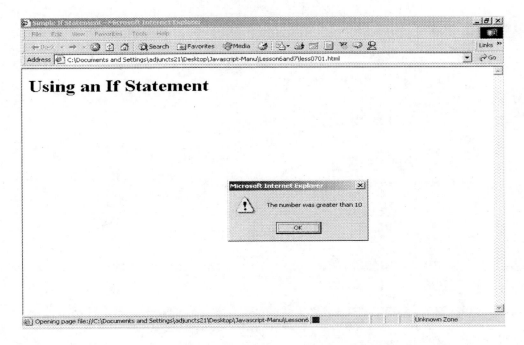

This code prompts the user to enter a number. The number entered by the user is stored in the variable number in numeric format by the JavaScript function parseInt. Refer to Lesson 04 for a description of how parseInt works.

Next the code performs a simple if statement. The number entered is compared with 10. If it is greater than 10, then and only then is an alert box displayed. Run the program a few times with numbers above 10 and below 10. If they are above 10, your code should display an alert box. If the number entered is below 10, it should do nothing. What happens when you enter 10 exactly?

Student Modifications

- Add an else clause to the if statement that displays an alert box with the message that the number was less than or equal to 10.

- Instead of comparing the input number to 10, prompt the user to enter two numbers and compare the first number to the second number, i.e. display either "The first number is greater than the second number," or " The first number is less than or equal to the second number," depending on the result of your comparison.

Save your code from the previous exercise and start a new HTML file. Save it using the name lesson0702.html.

Now type in **exactly** the following code:

```
1   <html>

2   <head>

3   <title>Testing the Temperature</title>
4   </head>

5   <body>

6   <h1>What is the temperature?</h1>

7   <script language="Javascript">

8   <!--

9   var temperature = parseFloat(prompt("Enter the outside temperature in
    Fahrenheit"," "));

10  document.write("You entered a temperature of ",temperature,"<br>");

11  if (temperature >=80)

12  {

13   document.write("It's hot!!! Wear your shorts!!!<br>");

14  }

15  else

16  {

17   document.write("It's not so hot!! Wear a sweater!!!<br>");

18  }

19  //-->

20  </script>

21  </body>

22  </html>
```

If you run this code and enter a value of 90, you will see this result:

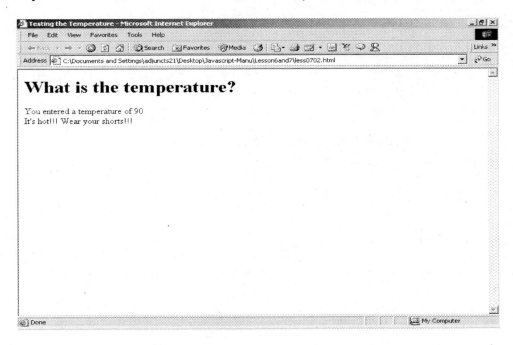

If you run this code, and enter a value of 50, you will see this result:

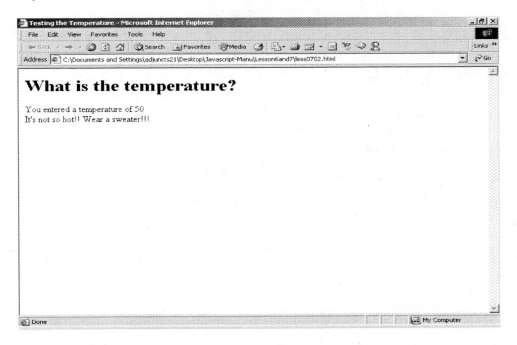

This code uses an if statement to test the value of the temperature. It prompts the user to enter a number, and converts the number to floating point format using the JavaScript function parseFloat. Recall from Lesson 04 that parseFloat stores numbers that can have a fractional value. Try this code a few times, entering both whole numbers and numbers with a fractional value. Enter the number 79.999. What is the result? Enter the number 80.001. What is the result?

Student Modifications

- Most of the world uses Celsius or Centigrade temperature values. What is considered a hot temperature in Centigrade? Re-write this program to ask the user to enter a Centigrade temperature. You also have to change the if statement to reflect a Centigrade value.

- Add additional if … else statements to test different levels of temperature. Here is what your if … else statements should look like:

```
if (temperature >= 100)

{

alert ("wow is it hot!")

}

else if (temperature >=90)

{

alert (.....)

}

else if ....
```

JavaScript Guessing Game

Now you will use the if statement in a guessing game. This program prompts the user to guess a number between 1 and 10. If the guess is correct, an alert box tells the user they guessed the right number. If it is not correct, the alert box tells the user they guessed the wrong number.

Save your code from the previous exercise and start a new HTML file. Save it using the name lesson0703.html.

Now type in *exactly* the follwing code:

```
1   <html>

2   <head>

3   <title>JavaScript Guessing Game</title>

4   <script language="Javascript">

5   <!—

6   function makeGuess()

7   { var guess = parseInt(prompt('Guess a number from 1 to 10', ' '));
```

```
8   if(guess == number)

9   alert('You guessed right :)')

10  else

11  alert('Wrong number guess again :(');

12  }

13  //-->

14  </script>

15  </head>

16  <body>

17  <center>

18  <h1>Guess The Right Number</h1>

19  <h2>Welcome to the guessing game!</h2>

20  <h2>Guess a number between 1 and 10</h2>

21  </center>

22  <script language="Javascript">

23  <!--

24  var number=(Math.floor(Math.random()*10))+1;

25  //-->

26  </script>

27  <center>

28  <input type="button" value="Make a Guess" onClick="makeGuess();">

29  </center>

30  </body>

31  </html>
```

This code is the start of a guessing game. It allows the user to make a guess. If you run this code and guess the wrong number, you get the following message:

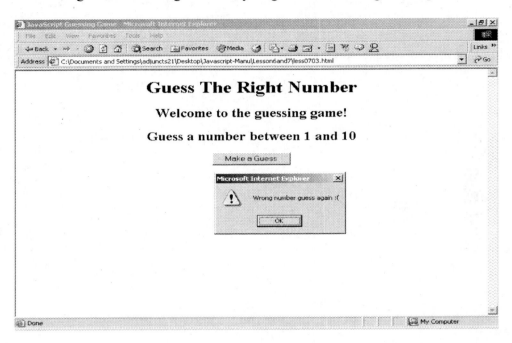

If you run this code and guess the correct number, you get this message:

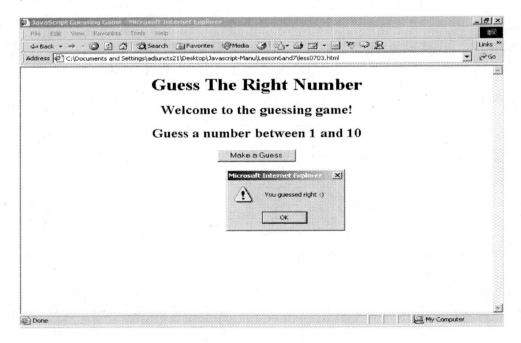

This code works in the following way.

The computer has to first "pick" the secret number for you to guess. It does this in the following line:

```
var number=(Math.floor(Math.random()*10))+1;
```

Although this code looks quite complicated, it is basically doing a simple thing – guessing a number from 1 to 10. In order to do this, it uses two JavaScript functions, **Math.random()** and **Math.floor()**. Math.random() is a special function that generates random numbers. Random numbers are very useful in computer science. They are used by many computer games, and can be used to simulate animation, and also to generate passwords.

Math.random() generates a random fractional number between the range of just above 0 (zero) up to 1. This code takes the fractional number from Math.random() and multiplies it by 10. This now expands the range of the random number from just above 0 (i.e. 0.256 or 0.889) to above 9 (i.e. 9.003, or 9.8761). It has the effect of stretching out the numbers from 0 to almost 1 to 0 to almost 10.

For our guessing game, we are not at all interested in any of those fractional values; we just want to chop them off. That is what Math.floor() does for us; it chops off any fractional numbers, leaving just the whole number, from 0 to 9. This is close to what we want. We now need to add 1 to make the range from 1 to 10. Once we have a number in this range, the assignment operator (=) stores it in the variable number.

After the computer has "picked" the secret number, the user makes a guess by clicking a button. The onClick event handler for that button now executes the makeGuess() function. Recall in the last lesson we learned that functions are often used with event handlers to respond to user events once the code becomes more than one or two lines. The makeGuess() function prompts the user to enter a number. It uses parseInt to store the user's number in numeric format in the variable guess. It then uses an if statement to compare guess with number. If they are equal, the user has guessed correctly; otherwise they have not guessed correctly.

This is just the start of the Guessing Game. Now we are going to start making some additions. After a few wrong guesses, you may get tired of the game and want to see what the right answer is. We will now add a button and a function to let the user see what the correct number is.

Add another button to this code in the line right after the first button by entering this code on a new line:

```
<input type="button" value="I Give Up!" onClick="showAnswer();">
```

Now you need to add the showAnswer() function to your code. Place this in the head section right after the closing brace of the makeGuess() function, but before the closing script tag (i.e. after line 12). Here is the code you should insert:

```
function showAnswer()

{

alert("The correct number is " + number);

}
```

If you run this code and click the "I give up!" button you will see the following display:

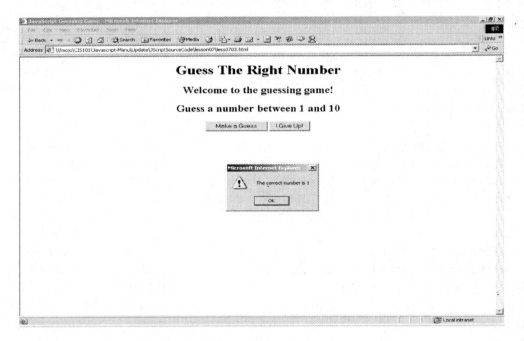

Student Modifications

- Provide a hint to the user if they guess the wrong number. Tell them if their guess was too high or too low. Use an if statement inside the makeGuess() function in order to do this. Be careful. Only give this hint if they guess the wrong number.

- Add a button with the value= "New Game" that changes the secret number. Add a new function rePlay() that re-sets the value of number. Place this code inside your function to reset the number

  ```
  number=(Math.floor(Math.random()*10))+1;
  ```

  Also display an alert message to the user to let them know they are starting a new game with a new number.

Key Terms and Definitions

- **branching or conditional statement** – A statement in a programming language that asks a question or determines a condition and executes different instructions depending on the answer.
- **if and if ... else statement** – if and if ... else are examples of conditional statements that are part of JavaScript. Both if and if ... else examine a condition. For the if statement, code is executed if the condition is true. For the if ... else statements, one block of code is executed if the condition is true and a separate block of code is executed if the condition is false.
- **comparison operators** – Operators that allow code to compare two values, and return a result of either true or false. The comparison operators available are == (equal), ! = (not equal), > (greater), >= (greater equal), < (less), and <= (less equal).
- **boolean values** – These are values that can have only two possible states: true or false.
- **if block** – section of code that is executed within an if statement if the tested condition is true.
- **else block** – Section of code that is executed within an if ... else statement if the tested condtion is false.
- **Math.random()** – JavaScript function that generates a random number.
- **Math.floor()** – JavaScript function that removes the fractional portion of a floating point number.

Lesson 7 Summary

The lesson taught you how to use conditional or branching statements. Conditional statements are a very important component of programming languages. Conditional statements ask a question, then execute different code depending on the answer. You learned that you can use the comparison operators to ask questions in JavaScript. Comparison operators compare two values, and return an answer of either true or false. You also learned that you can use the if and if ... else statements to branch to different code blocks depending on the result of a comparison. Finally, in the lab you used the if statement and comparison operators to create a simple guessing game.

Lesson 7 Exercises

7_1.   Write a program that inputs the number of items to be purchased and inputs the price per item, then prints the discounted price. The purchase is discounted by 15% only if there are 10 or more items purchased.

Prompt the user to input the number of items purchased and store it in a variable named numItems. Prompt the user to enter the price per item and store it in a variable price. Then use an if statement to determine if numItems is greater or equal to 10. If this is true, discount the price by 15%.

If total is a variable that contains the total cost of all the items, the code that applies the discount looks like this:

```
total = total * .85;
```

Display the total cost in an alert box. Include in the alert message to total cost and whether a discount was applied.

7_2.   Modify the previous program to allow a second level of discount of 25% for 50 items or more. Add another variable called discount, and set its value to .25 if they have purchased 50 or more items, .15 if they have purchased at least 10 to 49 items, and to 0 if they have purchased less than 10 items. Use the value in discount to calculate the final total and display it using an alert box. Include in the alert box the total amount due and the amount of the discount (if applicable).

7_3.   Using the previous programs as guides, create a page with JavaScript that asks in two prompt boxes for the quantity and the price, and then calculates and displays the total price including:

- no discount for totals below $100
- a 15% discount only if the total price exceeds $100.
- a 25% discount only if the total purchase exceeds $1000.
- a 30% discount only if the total purchase exceeds $10,000.

7_4.   Write a JavaScript program that prompts the user to enter their final average as a number. Use an if … else statement to display their grade as a letter equivalent, i.e. 90 or above is an A, 80 or above is a B, etc.

Lesson 8: Loops

OBJECTIVES: In this lesson you will learn about

- Loops

- The advantages of loops

- Increment and decrement operators

- For loop and while loop syntax

- Controlling loops with conditional expressions

Preparing to Program

One of the strongest features of a computer is its ability to repeat steps over and over as many times as is necessary without complaint or mistakes. For a computer, generating a payroll of 100 employees or 10,000 employees means doing the same thing 10,000 times rather than 100 times. It is not a hardship for a computer to repeat things over and over.

In this lesson , you will learn about JavaScript statements that command the computer to repeatedly execute a set of programming statements. The generic name for a programming statement that repeats is a **loop**. These statements are called loops because of the execution pattern they follow: they start at the beginning, execute all the statements that are to be repeated, go back to the top, and do it all over again. If you drew a line following this pattern, you would draw a series of circles or loops. The set of statements which is repeatedly executed is called the **body of the loop**.

We will examine two types of JavaScript loops: the **for** loop and the **while** loop. Before we explore the syntax of loops, you will learn about two operators used frequently with loops, the increment operator and the decrement operator.

The Increment and Decrement Operators

An important part of controlling a loop requires the computer to be able to count. For example, you may want to write a loop that repeats 40 times, so the computer needs to be able to count from 1 to 40. JavaScript has two operators to help with this. One adds +1 to a variable (the **increment operator**). This is useful when you want to count up to a certain value, i.e. 1, 2, 3. The other operator subtracts 1 (-1) from a variable (the **decrement operator**). This is useful when you want to count down to a certain value, i.e. 3, 2, 1.

The increment operator ++

The increment operator ++ is used with a variable, either prefix (before) or postfix (after).

The operator ++ increments the value of the variable by 1.

For example:

```
num++; //increases num by 1

++num; //increases num by 1
```

Both num++ and ++num increment the value of num by 1, but at different times (see below).

The decrement operator --

The decrement operator -- is used with a variable,
either prefix (before) postfix (after).

The decrement operator -- decreases the value of the variable by 1.

For example:

```
num--; //decreases num by 1

--num; //decreases num by 1
```

Both num-- and --num decrement the value of num by 1, but at different times (see below).

What is the difference between ++num and num++?

The difference between ++num and num++ is slight. For the programs you will write in CIS101, they behave in the same way, so you may skip this optional explanation if you wish.

The prefix operator, ++num, increments first and then uses the value of the variable num.
The postfix operator, num++, increments after using the value of the variable num.

Example

```
num=5;
document.write(num);        // prints 5
document.write(num++);      // prints 5, then adds one, so num becomes 6 after printing
document.write(num);        // prints 6
document.write(++num);      // prints 7 since it adds the one prior to printing
document.write(num);        // prints 7
```

You can avoid any confusion about the difference between ++num and num++ by only using the ++ operator in a simple statement, i.e. not combined with any other code like a write statement or an assignment statement.

Loops

Loops have the following structure:

loop test
//loop begins
{
body of the loop
}
loop ends

Loops have a test to determine whether the next iteration of the loop should proceed. Just like with the if statement, the test is a true false condition. You will use the same kinds of conditional expressions to control a loop as you did to control an if statement.

When the loop test proves true, the set of program commands in the body of the loop is executed again. When the test turns false, the loop terminates by skipping the body of the loop and continuing with the next command that follows the loop. With the loops we will use in CIS101, if the test is false the very first time, the loop is skipped and never entered.

This lesson will explain the syntax of two loop statements, the for loop and the while loop.

The for Loop

The **for** loop enables you to specify how many times the body of the loop will execute.

Syntax:
for (**expression1; expression2; expression3**)
{
statements to be repeated go here
}

where:
expression1 is used to initialize a variable (named the **control variable**).
expression2 is the loop test that determines whether the loop should continue.
expression3 is used to modify the value of the control variable.

The **for** statement is implemented using the following steps:

- step 1: initialize the control variable in *expression1*
- step 2: if *expression2* is **true,** execute the body of the loop.
- step 3: update the value of the control variable using *expression3.*
- Repeats steps 2 and 3, until *expression2* becomes **false.**

Example

```
for (n = 1; n <=100 ; n++) {
body of loop
}
```
Here n is the loop control variable, and the body of the loop will be repeated 100 times. In step 3, the value of n is increased by one through the use of the increment operator ++. You often use the increment operator ++ in this part of a for loop.

Notes

If the body of the loop has only one statement, the curly braces {...} can be omitted.

Traditionally, the control variables for loops are often i, j, k, etc. (This comes from languages like Fortran where they were the only variables allowed for counting loop iterations. Old habits die hard.)

Here is an example of code using a for loop that prints the numbers 1 through 10 to the screen. (Filename is less08_ex1.html):

```
1   <html>

2   <head>

3   <title>Using the For Loop</title>

4   </head>

5   <body>

6   <h1>The page uses a for loop to display 10 numbers</h1>

7   <script language="Javascript">

8   <!--

9   for (i = 1; i <=10 ; i++)

10  {

11  document.write("Here is the number: " + i + "<br>");

12  }

13  //-->

14  </script>

15  </body>

16  </html>
```

When you run this code, this is the output it produces:

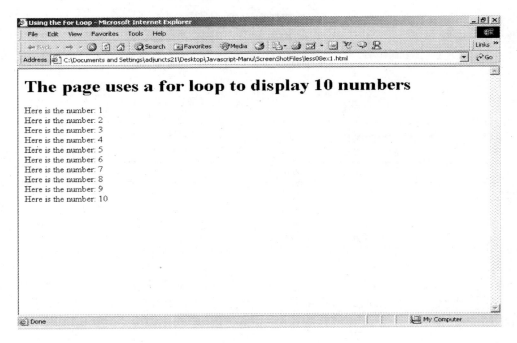

The while Loop

The next loop you will learn about in this lesson is the while loop. Here is the syntax of the while loop:

Syntax:
```
while (condition)
{
statements to be repeated
}
```
where *condition* is a true false test, the same as in the if statement and the for loop. The condition is tested to see whether it is true or false. If it is true, the body of the loop is executed. After all the statements in the body of the loop have been executed, the condition is tested again. If the condition is still true, the entire process is repeated (do the commands and loop back to test the condition). When the condition does become false, the body of the loop is not executed, and execution jumps to the statement that follows the loop. Thus, the body of the loop is repeatedly executed only as long as the *condition* remains true.

Example

```
n = 0

while (n <=100)

{
document.write(n)

n++

}
```

You can often use either a for loop or a while loop to produce the same result. Here is another example of JavaScript code that uses a while loop to print the numbers 1 through 10 on the screen. (Filename is less08_ex2.html):

```
1   <html>

2   <head>

3   <title>Using the While Loop</title>

4   </head>

5   <body>

6   <h1>The page uses a while loop to display 10 numbers</h1>

7   <script language="Javascript">

8   <!--

9   var i = 1;

10  while (i <=10)

11  {

12  document.write("Here is the number: " + i + "<br>");

13  i++;

14  }

15  //-->

16  </script>

17  </body>

18  </html>
```

If you execute this code, this will display on the screen:

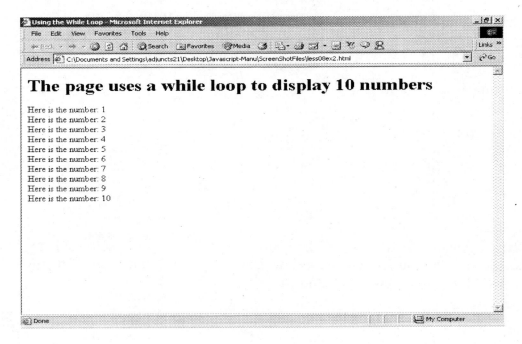

In the Lab

In this lesson you will learn to use loops.

Open Notepad and begin a new HTML document. Save it giving it the name lesson0801.html. You will also need to obtain from your instructor the image file star.gif, and save a copy of this file in the same folder as lesson0801.html.

Now type in *exactly* the following code:

```
<html>
1    <head>
2    <title>Writing Stars With a Loop</title>
3    </head>
4    <body>
5    <h1>This JavaScript Uses a Loop to Insert Stars on This Page</h1>
6    <script language="Javascript">
7    <!--
8    var num=parseInt(prompt("How many stars to display?", "10"));
9    for (i=1; i <=num; i++)
10   {
```

```
11 document.write("<img src='star.gif'>");

12 }

13 //-->

14 </script>

15 </body>

16 </html>
```

This code prompts the user for the number of stars they want to display. The default input value is 10. Then a for loop is executed beginning with the control variable i equal to 1, and ending when the control variable is equal to the number input by the user. Notice that the increment operator ++ is used to increment the control variable i. Also notice that image tags for each star are written to the document using the command document.write.

If you run this code with an input value of 7, you see the following output:

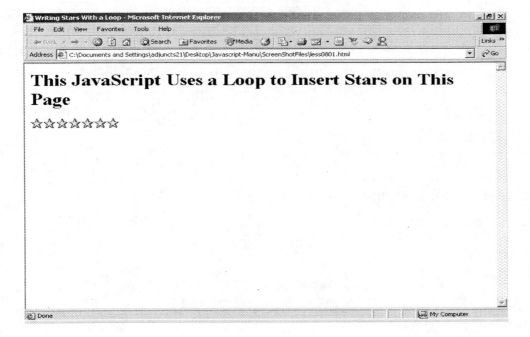

Student Modifications

- Execute your code with different values. Enter a value of 0. Enter a negative value. Enter a very large value, like 3,000.

- Find another image that you want to display. Insert another document.write statement to first display the star image and then to display the second image each time the loop body executes. To do this, repeat the document.write statement inside the body of the loop referencing the second image file. That second image file must also be loaded in the same folder as your code file, lesson0801.html.

- Rewrite this code using a while loop instead of a for loop. Which loop do you prefer to use?

Using Loops to Shake the Browser Window

You can use loops to shake your browser window. Save your work from the previous exercise and start a new file, and save it with the name lesson0802.html.

This code will only work with Internet Explorer 4.0 or above or Netscape 4 or above.

Now type in *exactly* the following code:

```
1   <html>

2   <head>

3   <title>JavaScript Shaking Screen</title>

4   <SCRIPT LANGUAGE="Javascript">

5   <!-- Begin

6   function shake(n)

7   {

8   for (i = 10; i > 0; i--)

9   {

10  for (j = n; j > 0; j--)

11  {

12  self.moveBy(0,i);

13  self.moveBy(i,0);

14  self.moveBy(0,-i);

15  self.moveBy(-i,0);
```

```
16  } //end inner loop

17  }// end outer loop

18  } //end function

19  // End -->

20  </script>

21  </head>

22  <BODY BGCOLOR="#CDCDCD" TEXT="#23238E" LINK="#FF2400"

23  VLINK="#FF2400" ALINK="#E6E8FA">

24  <h1>This only works with IE 4 or above or Netscape 4 or above</h1>

25  <p>

26  <form>

27  <input type=button onClick="shake(2)" value="Shake Screen"
    name="button">

28  </form>

29  </p>

30  </body>

31  </html>
```

Test this code by running it in a browser, and you will see your browser window shake when you click the button. This code uses two for loops, one inside the other, along with the function self.moveBy to shake the screen.

A loop inside a loop is called a nested loop. The loop on the outside is called the outer loop. The loop on the inside is called the inner loop.

The outer loop for this code controls how many times the window shakes altogether.

The inner loop controls how far in each direction (up and down, and left and right), your window shakes.

When you click the button you call a function shake with a parameter value of 2. This value is used by shake to control how much the window shakes.

Student Modifications

- Add a second button that calls the function shake with a different value for the parameter. Try it with different values, like 1, 5, or 10.

- You can add code that will shake your window as soon as it is loaded by using the **onLoad event handler**. The onLoad event is triggered when your page is loaded. Add the following event handler code to the body tag of your file:

```
onLoad = "shake(3);"
```

Key Terms and Definitions

- **loop** – A programming statement that repeats a set of statements. It is controlled by a test condition. The statements are repeated as long as the test condition is true. The loop ends when the test condition is false.
- **body of the loop** – The portion of a loop that is repeated.
- **for loop** – JavaScript statement that allows you to repeat a section of code a specified number of times.
- **while loop** – JavaScript loop statement that repeats a section of code as long as its test condition is true. The loop will terminate when the test condition is false.
- **increment operator** – JavaScript operator that increases the value of a variable by +1.
- **decrement operator** – JavaScript operator that decreses the value of a variable by –1.
- **control variable** – Variable used to control a loop. Once the control variable reaches or achieves a certain value, the loop is terminated.
- **nested loop** – One loop inside another loop is called a nested loop.
- **onLoad event handler** – Event handler that is part of the body tag. It is triggered when the Web page is loaded by the browser.

Lesson 8 Summary

In this lesson you have learned that programming languages have statements that allow the programmer to specify sections of code that can repeat over and over. You learned that these statements are called loops, because they continually loop back to the beginning of their code. You learned the syntax of two JavaScript loop statements, the for loop and the while loop. You also learned about the increment operator and the decrement operator, that are frequently used to control loops. Finally you learned how to use the onLoad event handler in order to trigger code as a Web page is being loaded by the browser.

Lesson 8 Exercises

8_1.   Create a Web page using JavaScript that displays all the even numbers between 1 and 100. Hint: create a variable num and set it equal to 2. Display its value using document.write, then add 2 to num each time you repeat the loop body. Keep on repeating until you reach 100.

8_2.   Create a page that prompts the user to enter a starting number and an ending number. Use a loop that displays all the numbers between the starting number and the ending number.

For example, if the user entered 5 as the starting number and 9 as the ending number, the output would look like this:

5
6
7
8
9

8_3.   Here is song you probably remember from long bus trips:

99 bottles of beer on the wall,
99 bottle of beer!
If one of those bottle should happen to fall,
98 bottle of beer on the wall.

98 bottle of beer ….

You can use a loop along with the decrement operator to write out the words to this song. Create a variable num and initialize it to 99. Create a series of document.write statements, one for each line in the song. But instead of including the actual number in the document.write statement, use the variable num.

For example, this code will display the first line of the first verse:

```
var num = 99;

document.write(num + " bottles of beer on the wall,<br>");
```

Before you write out the last line of the verse, add a statement that decreases the value in num, i.e. num--. Place all your document.write statements inside a loop. Be sure that the last verse displayed is for no (zero) bottles of beer.

Appendix A: JavaScript Reserved Words

The reserved words in this list cannot be used as JavaScript variables, functions, methods, or object names. Some of these words are keywords used in JavaScript; others are reserved for future use.

abstract	else	int	switch
boolean	extends	interface	synchronized
break	false	long	this
byte	final	native	throw
case	finally	new	throws
catch	float	null	transient
char	for	package	true
class	function	private	try
const	goto	protected	typeof
continue	if	public	var
default	implements	return	void
delete	import	short	while
do	in	static	with
double	instanceof	super	

Appendix B: Netscape Named Colors

You can use any of the following named colors in any JavaScript or HTML statement that uses a color. For example:

```
document.bgColor="cornflowerblue"
```

	Netscape Name	Value
Blues:	azure	F0FFFF
	aliceblue	F0F8FF
	lavender	E6E6FA
	lightcyan	E0FFFF
	powderblue	B0E0E6
	lightsteelblue	B0C4DE
	paleturquoise	AFEEEE
	lightblue	ADD8E6
	blueviolet	8A2BE2
	lightskyblue	87CEFA
	skyblue	87CEEB
	mediumslateblue	7B68EE
	slateblue	6A5ACD
	cornflowerblue	6495ED
	cadetblue	5F9EA0
	indigo	4B0082
	mediumturquoise	48D1CC
	darkslateblue	483D8B
	steelblue	4682B4
	royalblue	4169E1
	turquoise	40E0D0
	dodgerblue	1E90FF
	midnightblue	191970
	aqua	00FFFF
	cyan	00FFFF
	darkturquoise	00CED1
	deepskyblue	00BFFF
	darkcyan	008B8B
	blue	0000FF
	mediumblue	0000CD
	darkblue	00008B
	navy	000080

Greens:

Netscape Name	Value
mintcream	F5FFFA
honeydew	F0FFF0
greenyellow	ADFF2F
yellowgreen	9ACDC2
palegreen	98FB98
lightgreen	90EE90
darkseagreen	8FBC8F
olive	808000
aquamarine	7FFFD4
chartreuse	7FFF00
lawngreen	7CFC00
olivedrab	6B8E23
mediumaquamarine	66CDAA
darkolivegreen	556B2F
mediumseagreen	3CB371
limegreen	32CD32
seagreen	2E8B57
forestgreen	228B22
lightseagreen	20B2AA
springgreen	00FF7F
lime	00FF00
mediumspringgreen	00FA9A
teal	008080
green	008000
darkgreen	006400

Reds:

Netscape Name	Value
lavenderblush	FFF0F5
mistyrose	FFE4E1
pink	FFC0CB
lightpink	FFB6C1
orange	FFA500
lightsalmon	FFA07A
darkorange	FF8C00
coral	FF7F50
hotpink	FF69B4
tomato	FF6347
orangered	FF4500
deeppink	FF1493
fuchsia	FF00FF
magenta	FF00FF
red	FF0000
salmon	FA8072
lightcoral	F08080
violet	EE82EE
darksalmon	E9967A
plum	DDA0DD
crimson	DC143C
palevioletred	DB7093
orchid	DA70D6
thistle	D8BFD8
indianred	CD5C5C
mediumvioletred	C71585
mediumorchid	BA55D3
firebrick	B22222
darkorchid	9932CC
darkviolet	9400D3
mediumpurple	9370DB
darkmagenta	8B008B
darkred	8B0000
purple	800080
maroon	800000

Yellows:

Netscape Name	Value
ivory	FFFFF0
lightyellow	FFFFE0
yellow	FFFF00
floralwhite	FFFAF0
lemonchiffon	FFFACD
cornsilk	FFF8DC
gold	FFD700
khaki	F0E68C
darkkhaki	BDB76B

Browns:

Netscape Name	Value
snow	FFFAFA
seashell	FFF5EE
papayawhite	FFEFD5
blanchedalmond	FFEBCD
bisque	FFE4C4
mocassin	FFE4B5
navajowhite	FFDEAD
peachpuff	FFDAB9
oldlace	FDF5E6
linen	FAF0E6
antiquewhite	FAEBD7
beige	F5F5DC
wheat	F5DEB3
sandybrown	F4A460
palegoldenrod	EEE8AA
burlywood	DEB887
goldenrod	DAA520
tan	D2B48C
chocolate	D2691E
peru	CD853F
rosybrown	BC8F8F
darkgoldenrod	B8860B
brown	A52A2A
sienna	A0522D
saddlebrown	8B4513

Grays:

Netscape Name	Value
white	FFFFFF
ghostwhite	F8F8FF
whitesmoke	F5F5F5
gainsboro	DCDCDC
lightgray	D3D3D3
silver	C0C0C0
darkgray	A9A9A9
gray	808080
lightslategray	778899
slategray	708090
dimgray	696969
darkslategray	2F4F4F
black	000000